The Best Of *The Mailbox*® Math

Preschool-Kindergarten

W9-AXQ-261

Editors
Jayne Gammons
Kim T. Griswell

Artists
Teresa R. Davidson, Nick Greenwood, Sheila Krill, Barry Slate

Cover Artist
Jennifer Tipton Bennett

©1998 by THE EDUCATION CENTER, INC.
All rights reserved.
ISBN #1-56234-265-7

Manufactured in the United States
10 9 8 7 6 5 4 3 2 1

About This Book

You can count on *The Best Of* The Mailbox® *Math* to provide you with the ideas you'll need to teach youngsters the basics of mathematics. The ideas have been compiled from the 1990 to 1995 issues of *The* Preschool/Kindergarten *Mailbox®* magazine. Inside you'll find math units, literature connections, learning centers, games, and tips. We've also included an easy-to-use index so that you can locate ideas by math skills. It all adds up to marvelous math fun!

Table Of Contents

Math Units

GEOMETRIC GYM

When it's time to get into shapes, visit this gym for a thorough workout with circles, squares, rectangles, and triangles.

by Lucia Kemp Henry

Shapes

Shapes can help us every day.
We use shapes for work and play.
Square, circle, rectangle—triangle too!
Look and find the shapes—all around you.

A square is a place to lay your head. *(a pillow)*
A square is a scarf that's colored red. *(a bandana)*
Squares let the sun in, bright as can be. *(a window)*
Squares on the floor make patterns you see. *(tiles)*

A triangle's a sign for cars in the street. *(a yield sign)*
A triangle's a slice of something to eat. *(a pizza slice)*
Triangles are hats for party fun. *(a party hat)*
Camp in a triangle when the day is done. *(a tent)*

A circle can roll along the ground. *(a tire)*
A circle can bounce up and down. *(a ball)*
A circle is a fresh, tasty pie. *(a pie)*
A circle is something in the sky. *(the sun)*

A rectangle is a frame for something pretty. *(a picture frame)*
A rectangle holds shoes for country or city. *(a shoebox)*
Rectangles are places for fish to stay. *(an aquarium)*
You can play football on a rectangle today. *(a football field)*

—*by Lucia Kemp Henry*

Working Out With What's Available

Use this rhyming riddle to introduce your youngsters to the shapes around them. Before sharing the rhyme with your students, use a photocopier to enlarge the picture cards on page 10. Then color and cut apart the cards along the grid lines. If desired, prepare these illustrated cards for flannelboard use. When sharing the rhyme with students, have youngsters scan the picture cards and locate an illustration to match each clue given in lines 5 through 20.

Flip-The-Shapes Booklet

As a follow-up activity to the poem above, help your youngsters complete these small flip booklets. Reproduce the flip booklet cover and booklet pages (on pages 10–14) in classroom quantities. Using a paper cutter, cut along the bold outlines; then give each student a copy of each booklet page, the front cover, and a plain back cover (7 1/4" x 4 3/4"). Have each student color the book's components as he desires. Then have each child cut along the dotted lines and stack the four half-pages with the labeled shapes in one pile and the 12 half-pages with the picture shapes in another pile. Provide assistance as each child staples his two sets of booklet half-pages (as shown) between the covers of his booklet. Encourage youngsters to flip the pages to find ones with corresponding shapes.

TRDavidson

Exercise Your Brain

Designate a table for the display of geometrically shaped objects. Cover the tabletop with bulletin-board paper; then have students sponge-print circles, triangles, squares, and rectangles all over the paper. Ask students to bring in objects that are similar in shape to any of the sponge-printed shapes. As objects begin to collect on the table, give students opportunities to manipulate and name the shapes before sorting them into groups by shape.

Secret Shapes

Play this question-and-answer game with the table full of objects collected in "Exercise Your Brain." Ask a few youngsters to stand at the shape table. Decide secretly on an object to be the focus of the first round of play. Have the youngsters at the table try to determine the object you have selected by asking a series of questions that can be answered with yes or no responses. Encourage students to begin with questions that will help them pinpoint the basic shape of the object you've selected. They might ask, for example, "Is the secret shape a circle [triangle, square, rectangle]?" As objects are eliminated by your responses, have students remove them from the table. Encourage students to continue by asking questions related to color, size, and purpose until only one object—the one you originally selected—remains on the table. Continue the game by replacing all the items on the table and secretly selecting (or having a child secretly select) an item to be the object for the next series of questions.

Which One Is Missing?

Use the items collected in "Exercise Your Brain" as supplies for this game. Arrange some objects in a line on a small table. After showing the group of objects to your students, ask youngsters to close their eyes while you remove one of the items. When students open their eyes, ask them to determine which item is missing. Encourage students to use both the name and the shape of the object when specifying what's missing.

I found a magic triangle. It was able to change itself into anything like gold, or peppermint, or plastic. The magic shape said, "Take me with you." So I did. I used the shape to play music during free time and to play catch on the playground.

Getting Into Shapes—Like Magic!

Spark imagination and creative thinking with "magical" shapes. To prepare for this activity, cut large, colorful sheets of paper into oversize circles, squares, triangles, and rectangles. Set the stage for this activity by asking each student to choose a shape cutout and to pretend that it is magical. Then have each child, in turn, dictate completions for the following incomplete thoughts: "I found a magic…," "It was…," "The magic shape said,….," and "I used the shape to…." Using a colorful marker or metallic pen, write each student's dictation on his shape cutout.

I found a magic circle. It was able to grant wishes. The magic circle said, "You can have three wishes." I used the shape to wish for a new baseball hat, a trip to the amusement park, and a puppy.

The Creative Approach To Shaping Up

After your students have completed their stories about the magical shapes described in "Getting Into Shapes—Like Magic," give them an opportunity to make collages to display with the stories. To make a corresponding collage, start with a shape cutout to match the one bearing the story and glue it to art paper. Then use paint and a sponge of the same shape to sponge-print the paper and the shape. Glue on small gift-wrap cutouts to match the large shape. Use glitter and shape stickers to add the finishing touches to the shape collages. Display each student's collage with his dictated story from "Getting Into Shapes—Like Magic!" (page 7).

My Circle Book by Jacob

Shape Minibooklets

After you introduce a shape, wouldn't it be nice to send each youngster home with a small shape booklet? On colorful paper, duplicate multiple copies of shape designs for minibooklets. Have parent volunteers assist you by cutting out each copy of the shapes and stapling them into booklets. After you have introduced a shape, present each student with a copy of the corresponding shape minibooklet, and have him personalize its cover. To fill each page, have each student draw, glue on, or sponge-print an object shaped similarly to the booklet. If desired, students may write, copy, or dictate a label for each page, before taking the minibooklets home to share with their families.

Muscle Vests

Prepare brown paper grocery bags in advance for this activity. You'll need a bag for each child. Cut head and arm holes from each bag, and cut a slit up one side of the bag to create the basic vest shape. Provide paint and sponges that have been cut into circles, triangles, rectangles, and squares. Ask students to use these supplies to decorate the fronts and backs of their paper vests. If desired, have each child color, cut out, and glue on matching shape button cutouts. Wearing these "shapely" vests, students can march around the room singing a shape song like the one that follows.

Shaping Up To Music

Cooperation is important as youngsters strengthen their shape-recognition skills using this activity. Make a giant, imitation rubber band from 1/2-inch-wide elastic sewn into a loop. As you sing each verse of the shape song below, have several students stand within the confines of the giant rubber band to create a likeness of the featured shape.

ice-cream cone

Shapes

(Each verse of this song is sung to the tune of "London Bridge Is Falling Down.")

Two sides long and two sides short.
Two sides short. Two sides short.
Two sides long and two sides short.
We're a rectangle!

We're as round as we can be.
We can be. We can be.
We're as round as we can be.
We're a circle.

We've got three corners and three sides.
See our sides, with your eyes.
We've got three corners and three sides.
We're a triangle.

Our four sides are just the same.
Just the same. Just the same.
Our four sides are just the same.
We're a square.

—by Shelley Rubin

Shelley Rubin—Preschool, St. Andrew Preschool, Lynchburg, VA

8

"Martin-izing" Shapes

If your students love Bill Martin, Jr.'s *Brown Bear, Brown Bear, What Do You See?*— and who doesn't?—they'll love this shape spin-off. Read aloud *Brown Bear, Brown Bear, What Do You See?*, and tell students that they will be making a similar book that contains shapes instead of animals. For the first page of the book, write, "Red circle, red circle, What do you see?" near the bottom of a sheet of paper. Program the second page of the book with something like, "I see a green rectangle looking at me." "Green rectangle, green rectangle, What do you see?" Continue programming any number of pages in a similar manner. When the pages have been programmed, pass each student a page and help him read the words. Then have him choose a shape from a collection you have provided or cut out and color one of his own and glue it to the page. Provide a final page that has a class photo and the words, "I see some boys and girls looking at me." Assemble and bind the booklet, and place it where youngsters can read it at their leisure.

Nina Tabanian—Gr. K, St. Rita School, Dallas, TX

Red circle, red circle, What do you see?

Spotlighting Shapes

Here's a game that encourages shaping up! In preparation for the game, tape cutouts of basic shapes around your classroom. Put some on the walls, some on the doors, some on the floor, and even some on the ceiling. Then darken the room somewhat and give a flashlight to a child. Have him shine the light on a shape and identify the shape. Then have him shine the flashlight beam on shapes that match the one he originally identified. After a while, have the student pass the flashlight to another student, and repeat the process until each child has had a turn. Vary the routine, if desired, by calling out the names of shapes one after another as the student holding the flashlight illuminates a shape to match each one you named.

Jeannie Ryan—Gr. K, Provident Heights, Waco, TX

Food For Champions

When you're really into shapes, you'll have something to celebrate. So consider culminating this unit with a party featuring snacks in the four basic shapes. For the party, cut student-made sandwiches into triangles, serve graham-cracker squares spread with peanut butter, top round crackers with cheese spread, and serve rectangular wafer cookies for dessert. As they chow down, encourage youngsters to comment on the shapes that they are eating.

Books To Really Help Youngsters Shape Up

Brown Rabbit's Shape Book
Written & Illustrated by Alan Baker
Published by Kingfisher Books

Afro-Bets®: Book Of Shapes
Written by Margery W. Brown & Illustrated by Culverson Blair
Published by Just Us Books

My Very First Book Of Shapes
Written & Illustrated by Eric Carle
Published by HarperCollins Children's Books

Shapes, Shapes, Shapes
Written & Photographed by Tana Hoban
Published by Greenwillow Books

Circles, Triangles, And Squares
Written & Photographed by Tana Hoban
Published by Macmillan Publishing Company, Inc.

The Shape Of Me And Other Stuff
Written & Illustrated by Dr. Seuss
Published by Random House, Inc.

Picture Cards
Use with "Working Out With What's Available" on page 6.

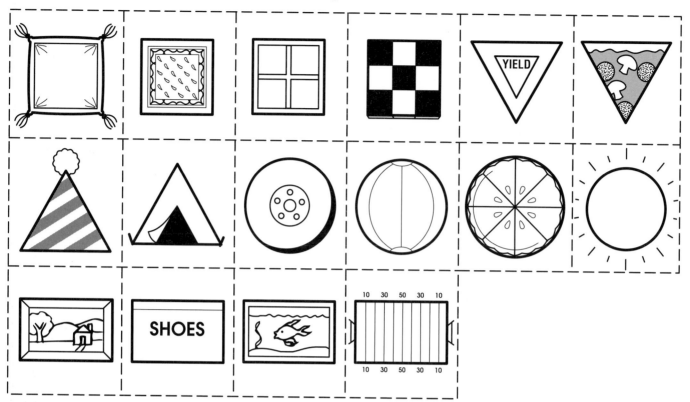

Flip Booklet Cover
Use with "Flip-The-Shapes Booklet" on page 6.

Flip the pages. Match each object on the bottom to its matching shape on the top.

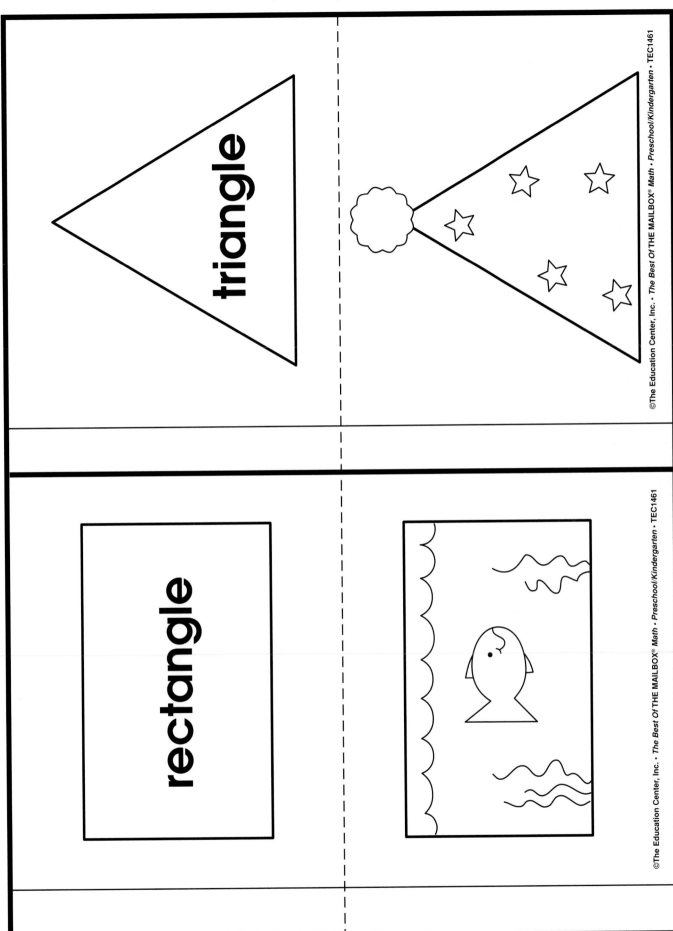

triangle

rectangle

Use with "Flip-The-Shapes Booklet" on page 6.

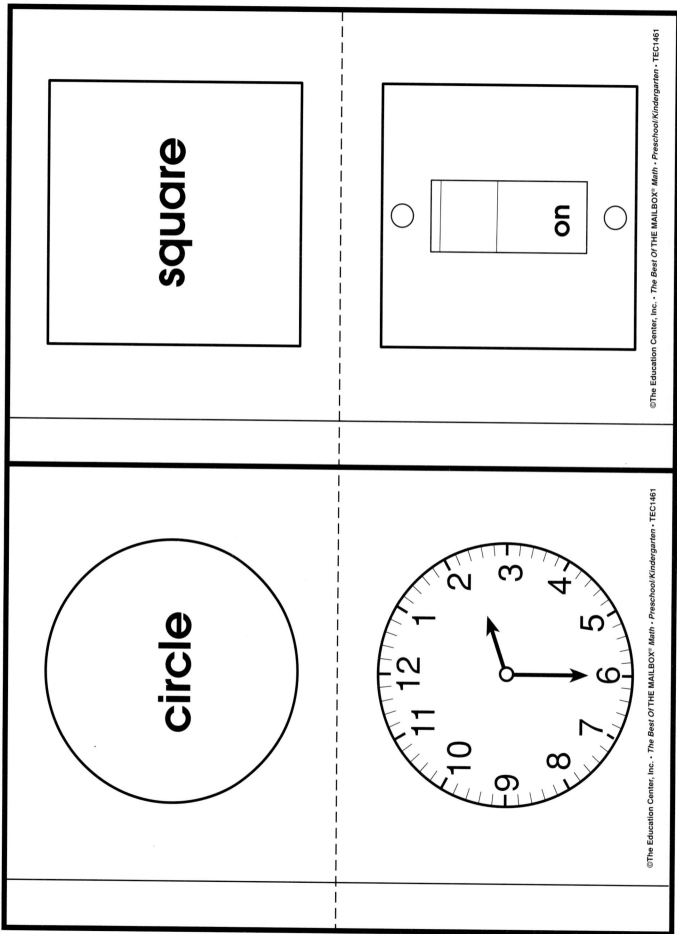

square

on

circle

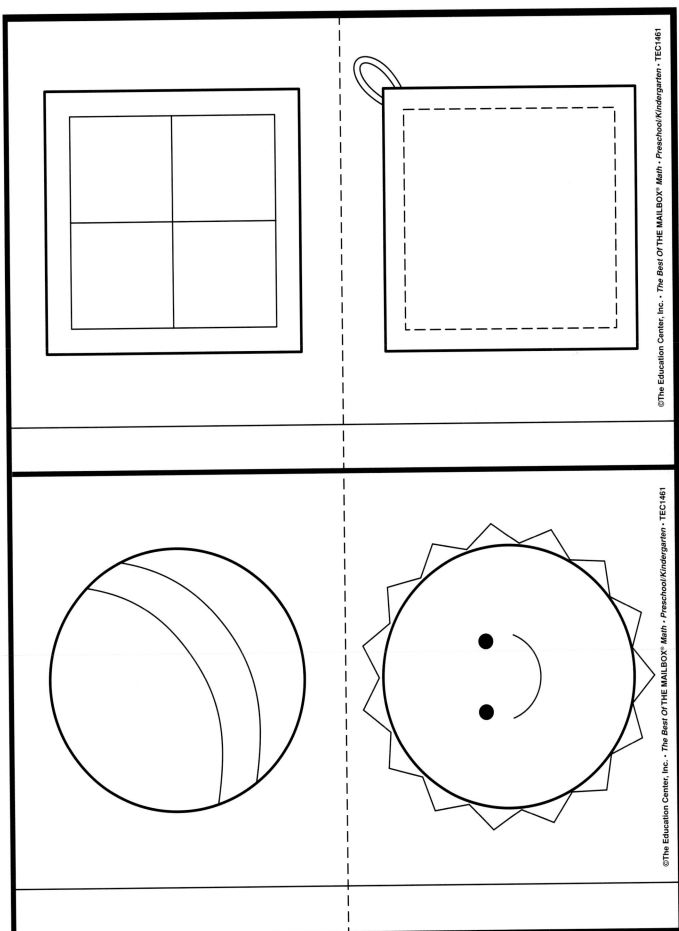

YIELD

Shoes

Getting Into Shapes!

When it comes to knowing basic geometric shapes, your students will be in good shape after playing these games!

Shape Strips

Play this shape-recognition game with small groups or the whole class. Cut out sets of shapes each containing a square, circle, oval, rectangle, and triangle from colored construction paper. You will need one set for each player, plus one additional set. Glue one set of shapes on a poster-board circle. Laminate and attach a spinner. Glue each remaining set of shape cutouts to a sentence strip.

To play, each player gets a shape strip and a button. Players take turns spinning the spinner and naming the shape. Players move their buttons to the shapes that are called.

Susie Fendley—Gr. K
Flowers School
Montgomery, AL

Shape Scavenger Hunt

Do your children go on a shape hunt in their classroom when learning basic shapes? Extend the activity by having a shape hunt in books. Give each child a sheet of tracing paper, and have him trace the shapes he finds in the illustrations of his favorite stories.

Patsy G. Higdon
Glen Arden Elementary School
Arden, NC

Shape Toss

Shapes are on target for a beanbag toss. Draw a teddy bear holding many balloons on a large piece of poster board. On each balloon, draw one basic, geometric shape. Color and laminate the poster board. Place the poster board on the floor and provide players with several beanbags. Players toss the beanbags and name the shapes the beanbags land on. To vary, have the child name a shape and try to toss the beanbag on that shape.

Giant Shape Dominoes

In this game of giant, shape dominoes, students string shapes together to cover the classroom floor! Use 9" x 12" sheets of black construction paper to make a large set of dominoes. Cut out basic shapes from colored construction paper. Paste two shapes on each black sheet, as shown. Laminate shape dominoes. Place one domino on the floor. Deal out the other dominoes. In turn, students try to put a matching shape adjacent to one on the floor. If a student doesn't have a matching shape, he misses a turn.

Counting With Celia And Cyrus

by Julie Kleinberger

You can count on your fingers.
You can count on every star.
But if you count all our legs,
You really count far!

Kick off some grand counting activities with Celia and Cyrus Centipede. These hands-on suggestions have been designed to improve your youngsters' self-esteem, as well as their counting skills.

Sing Along With Centipedes

Convert a pair of wild-and-tacky socks into centipede puppets to lead this sing-along, count-along song. To make the puppets, one female and one male, decorate a pair of socks using felt, yarn, and zany accessories such as gaudy earrings and a neon bow tie. Don your centipede puppets and teach your youngsters the song below. At the end of the verse, have a youngster designate something to count and don a centipede puppet for the counting. For example, youngsters may count the number of children wearing blue jeans, belts, or green shirts. You'll have a grand time singing and counting along!

One, Two, Three, Four, Five!

(sung to the tune of "Old MacDonald Had A Farm")

Celia Centipede likes to count.
One, two, three, four, five.
Cyrus Centipede likes to count.
Six, seven, eight, nine, ten.
They count things here.
They count things there.
Here they count, there they count,
Everywhere they count, count.
Name something that they can count.
One, two, three, four, five!

You did a good job of taking turns on the playground.

What nice manners you have.

Mrs. Cole said you were great listeners.

You did such a nice job of cleaning up your desks.

You were quiet as mice in the hall!

Centipede Compliment Counters

Before introducing this centipede display to the class, attach two construction paper strips (legs) to each of several paper circles or thin paper plates. Each time your class receives a compliment or reaches a goal, make a note of it on a circle or plate, before attaching it to a wall near your youngsters' eye level. Periodically, count the number of centipede sections and the number of legs. You'll see your students' dependability grow right along with their counting skills.

Counting On Kids

Youngsters will acknowledge that they are dependent on adults, but do they realize adults depend on them, too? Have each youngster give paper doll cutouts (page 18) to two adults who know him well, asking them to complete the form. Have each youngster attach his completed paper dolls to a classroom or hallway wall with those of his classmates. As your collection grows, have students count the paper dolls. They may be surprised to realize that adults count on kids, too.

Paper doll figures, each labeled "I can count on":

- Susan — to help pick up her toys. — Mom
- Derrick — to feed his cat Scruffy. — Dad
- Beth — to help set the table. — Grandma
- Tiffany — to brush her teeth every day. — Diane
- Jason — to help with the baby. — Mom

Centipede Center

Cutting corners can become a positive learning experience in this hands-on counting center. Provide horizontally halved sentence strips or 24" x 1 1/2" paper strips, 3"-square pieces of construction paper, 1/4" x 1" yellow paper rectangles, glue, markers, and scissors. If desired, display a series of Polaroid® pictures at the center to illustrate the steps for making a centipede. To make a centipede at the center, a student trims the corners from eight squares and glues the resulting circular pieces to a 24" strip. (An avid counter may want to attach two strips together.) Using markers, he then draws a face on his centipede, before gluing two or more yellow rectangles to each circle for the centipede's legs. When the centipede is complete, the youngster counts to find out how many body sections and legs his centipede has.

Stand Up And Be Counted!

Your students will beam with pride when you let them know their opinions count. Laminate an oversize grid for a reusable graph. Also glue a photocopy of each youngster's school picture to a duplicate of the pattern on page 18. Each week, post and discuss a pertinent question for students to answer. To respond, each youngster places his picture in the correct column on the grid to reflect his preference. Have youngsters count and compare the responses; then follow through with the most popular choice.

The "I Can" Can

Your students will flip their lids for this counting idea. In advance, ask youngsters to donate lidded, plastic, lemonade and beverage mix cans. Label a can for each youngster. On pastel paper, duplicate copies of the "I Can" form on page 18. On a copy of the "I Can" form, have each youngster copy a word or picture clue representing the item to be counted. Then have him count and write the appropriate number, before storing the form in his can. Each time a student flips his can lid to include another completed form, he'll be chalking up another counting experience.

Graph:

Where should we go on our field trip?		
...m	hospital	bakery

I can count
There are 2

Sally

Use with "Counting On Kids" on page 17.

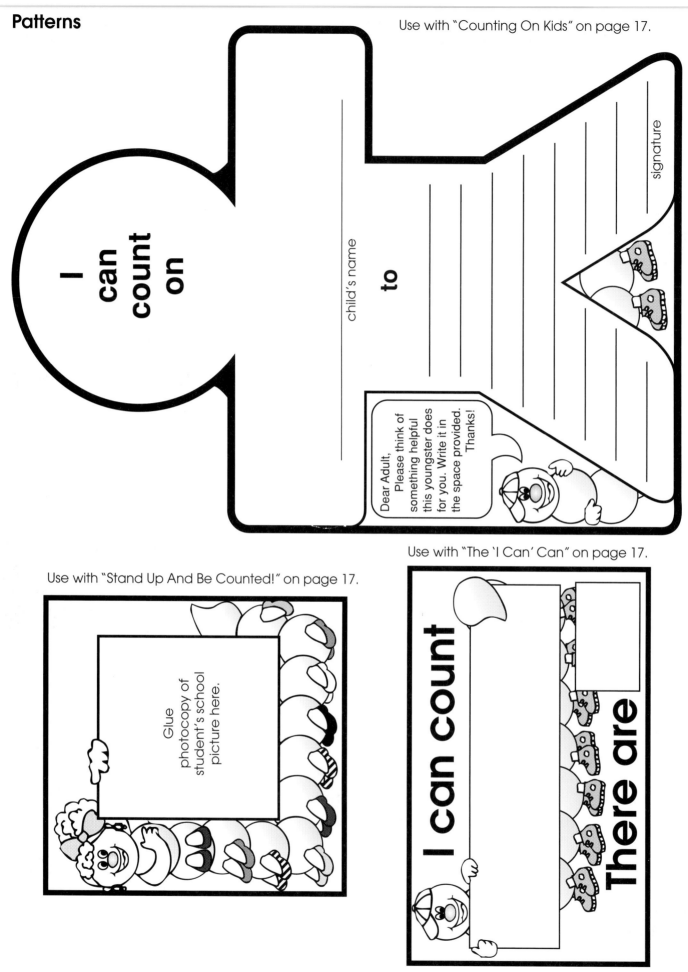

I can count on

child's name

to

signature

Dear Adult,
Please think of something helpful this youngster does for you. Write it in the space provided. Thanks!

Use with "The 'I Can' Can" on page 17.

I can count

There are

Use with "Stand Up And Be Counted!" on page 17.

Glue photocopy of student's school picture here.

TEACHING MATH WITH DOMINOES

Dig out that old set of dominoes or make your own domino set by putting sticky dots on sets of cardboard rectangles. Use dominoes alone or with other manipulatives to teach these math skills.

ideas by Patsy Higdon

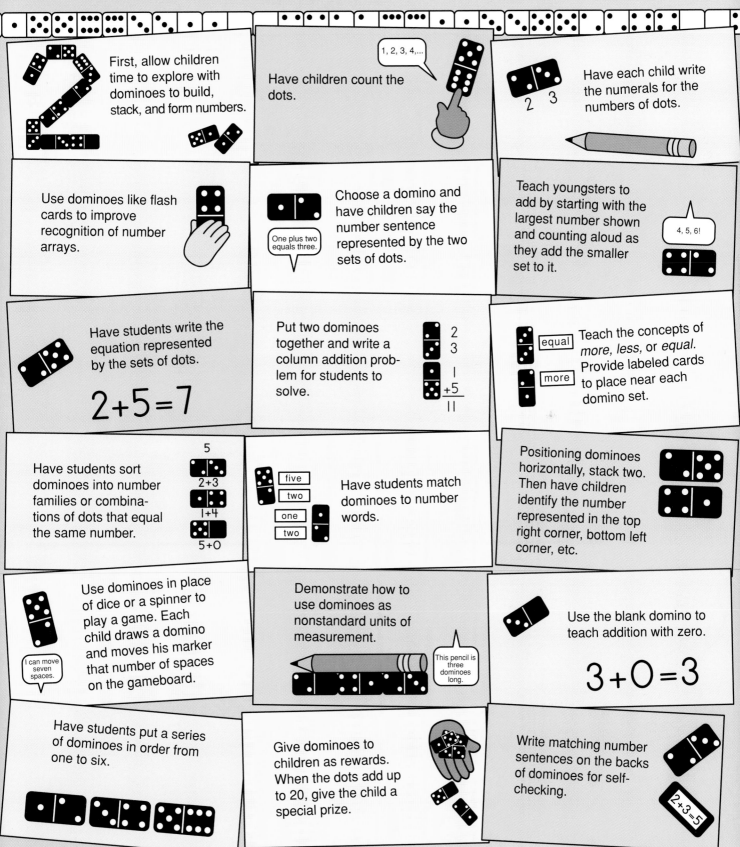

First, allow children time to explore with dominoes to build, stack, and form numbers.

Have children count the dots.

1, 2, 3, 4,...

Have each child write the numerals for the numbers of dots.

2 3

Use dominoes like flash cards to improve recognition of number arrays.

Choose a domino and have children say the number sentence represented by the two sets of dots.

One plus two equals three.

Teach youngsters to add by starting with the largest number shown and counting aloud as they add the smaller set to it.

4, 5, 6!

Have students write the equation represented by the sets of dots.

$2+5=7$

Put two dominoes together and write a column addition problem for students to solve.

2
3

1
+5
11

Teach the concepts of *more*, *less*, or *equal*. Provide labeled cards to place near each domino set.

equal

more

Have students sort dominoes into number families or combinations of dots that equal the same number.

5
2+3
1+4
5+0

Have students match dominoes to number words.

five
two
one
two

Positioning dominoes horizontally, stack two. Then have children identify the number represented in the top right corner, bottom left corner, etc.

Use dominoes in place of dice or a spinner to play a game. Each child draws a domino and moves his marker that number of spaces on the gameboard.

I can move seven spaces.

Demonstrate how to use dominoes as nonstandard units of measurement.

This pencil is three dominoes long.

Use the blank domino to teach addition with zero.

$3+0=3$

Have students put a series of dominoes in order from one to six.

Give dominoes to children as rewards. When the dots add up to 20, give the child a special prize.

Write matching number sentences on the backs of dominoes for self-checking.

2+3=5

"Mathe-magic"

Wave your magic wand and dazzle your audience with these sleight-of-hand "tricks" which sharpen number-recognition skills quicker than you can say, "Abracadabra!"

Ideas by Betty Silkunas, Lansdale, PA

Money Magic

You can count on this "trick" to add a little magic to number recognition. Turn 11 brightly colored plastic cups upside down; then program them with the numbers *zero* through *ten*. Begin the "trick" by displaying four of the cups on a table before the audience, then lifting each one to show there is nothing beneath it. Have youngsters cover their eyes and slowly turn around one time as you cry, "Hocus-pocus!" and quickly slide a coin under one of the cups. Then have youngsters guess which numbered cup is hiding the coin. The first youngster to guess correctly places another numbered cup atop the table and performs the trick for his classmates.

Feeling Is Believing

Smooth out the rough spots of number recognition with this sensory sensation. Using cardboard patterns, trace and cut out each of the numbers *zero* through *nine* from both sandpaper and poster board. Glue each sandpaper cutout atop its matching poster board counterpart. Place the cutouts inside an old top hat or "magic bag." Then blindfold a volunteer from the audience and ask him to draw a number. Wave your "magic wand" above him as you say, "Alakazam!" Then have him amaze the audience by feeling the cutout and revealing its identity.

Jumbled Jump Ropes

Untangle the mystery of numbers with this jewel of a "trick." Place a pile of three jumbled jump ropes on the floor. Whisper different numbers to three volunteers before each grabs a rope and starts jumping. As you wave your "magic wand" above their heads and exclaim, "Jumpin' jelly beans!" have the volunteers use their ropes to form the numbers that were whispered to them. Then have them select classmates, who can correctly identify the mystery numbers, to take their places.

Disappearing Numbers

Watch youngsters' number-recognition skills magically appear before your eyes with this fast-paced activity! Place a pail of *disappearing ink* (water) containing three large paintbrushes on the floor under the chalkboard. Using the disappearing ink, paint a number on the chalkboard. Have audience members hold up an equal number of fingers. Then select three volunteers, who are holding up the correct number of fingers, to paint the number on the chalkboard before yours "magically" disappears.

Magic Number Potion

Proceed with caution when you make this potion! Even small doses have been known to increase youngsters' number recognition! Begin by labeling a box containing large cups with the number *one*. Then label a box of straws with the number *two* and a gallon carton of vanilla ice cream with the number *three*. Fill three clean pump dispensers with three different kinds of juice or Kool-Aid; then label them with the numbers *four* through *six*. Assemble all items numerically on a table. Have each youngster take *one* cup and place *two* straws in it. Have him count along with you as you place *three* small scoops of ice cream in his cup; then have him count aloud as he pumps juice from each dispenser (the indicated number of times) into his cup. Have youngsters stir and sip their potion while trying to guess its mysterious ingredients.

DISAPPEARING NUMBERS

Missing Card Trick

Dazzle your audience with this mystifying card trick. Remove the *2, 4, 6, 8,* and *10* of clubs and the *3, 5, 7,* and *9* of hearts from a standard deck of playing cards, putting the remaining cards aside. Shuffle the designated cards and place them facedown atop a table. Choose a volunteer to select and conceal a card. Turn the remaining cards faceup and mystify onlookers as you quickly identify the missing card. Then reshuffle the cards and have the volunteer select another willing participant and perform the trick himself.

Dazzling Doubles

"Mathe-magicians" will be hoppin' for a chance to try a little matching magic. Program the backs of 11 matching pairs of cotton-covered bunny cutouts with the numbers *zero* through *ten* as shown. Place the programmed cutouts in a "magic" hat or bag. Select a volunteer to draw a cutout; then have him select another volunteer to come forward; say the magic word, "Abracadabra!"; and attempt to draw the matching cutout. If the cutout does not match, replace it and have another volunteer try again. Volunteers continue in this manner until all bunny pairs have been matched.

"En-light-ening" Numbers

Shed some light on number-recognition skills with this bright "trick." Use a hole puncher to punch the shapes of the numbers *zero* through *ten* in index card halves. Darken the room; then hold a card in front of a flashlight or other light source to project the punched number on a screen or wall. Have each observer who can identify the projected number signify by folding his arms across his chest and nodding his head. Call on an observer to identify the mystery number; then, if he identifies it correctly, have him select and project another one on the screen.

Now You See It; Now You Don't

As youngsters become master "mathe-magicians," try this hands-on activity. Using a washable marker, randomly label each child's fingers with the numbers *one* through *ten*. Select a "mathe-magician" to attempt to baffle the audience by bending one of his fingers down and challenging a selected onlooker to identify the missing number. The "mathe-magician" continues baffling the audience with additional finger "tricks" until the audience member he selects identifies the missing number. Whoever correctly identifies the missing number tries his hand at being the "mathe-magician."

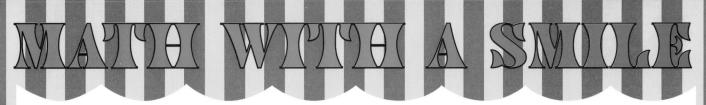

These hands-on activities will have your students eating, measuring, hugging, dressing up, and smiling through memorable math lessons.

Measure Up!

This cooperative learning activity allows every child to measure up. Divide your class into several groups. Give each group a different color of bulletin-board paper. Have each group spread the paper on the floor and trace the outline of one person onto the paper. Groups may decorate their figures and cut them out. Have group members take turns measuring the arms, legs, head, and body with various nonstandard units of measurement. Display the cutouts on a bulletin board and compare measurements.

Terri Fuzy—Gr. K
Evans Elementary School
Evans, GA

Eat 'Em Up!

Your students will have fun eating their way through this math lesson! Let each child dip into a bowl of Cheerios® with a spoon and count the number of Cheerios® in one spoonful. Then have each child roll a die to find out how many Cheerios® to eat. Finally, have each child count the number of Cheerios® left. Vary this activity by changing the size of the spoon, providing several dice to roll, or having the children work the problems either orally or on paper.

Weda Lee—Gr. K
Richland Elementary School
Richland, MS

Hug A Bear!

Children love learning ordinal numbers with huggable teddy bears. Place several teddy bears or other stuffed animals on a row of chairs. Give directions such as "Hug the third stuffed animal" or "Wiggle the fifth animal's nose." Math can feel good too!

Karen Martin—Gr. K, Hahira Elementary School, Hahira, GA

An Armful Of Bangles

Colorful plastic bracelets are perfect to reinforce number sequence. Purchase several wide plastic bangle bracelets and label each one with a numeral or a set of dots. Allow children to slip the bracelets on their arms in sequence.

Heather Harrison, Scarborough, Ontario, Canada

M&M's Math

Count the smiles when you use M&M's® candies to teach subtraction. Give each child five candies. On the board, write "five minus one." Ask each child to eat just one candy. Complete the number sentence on the board after asking youngsters to count their remaining candies. Begin a new problem with the number *four* and continue writing number sentences until all of the M&M's® are gone. To vary the activity, use Reese's Pieces® or popcorn for further subtraction practice.

Cathy Craze, Summersville, WV

Mr. Minus

Mr. Minus is a clown who teaches children to subtract. To become Mr. Minus, just put on a wig and a clown hat and carry a bunch of balloons into your classroom. Announce, "I'm Mr. Minus, and I like to take things away." Count the balloons aloud with your students, and then pop one balloon with a large knitting needle. Ask children how many balloons are left and write the corresponding number sentence on the board. Read the problem and identify the minus sign. Have students read the number sentence together. Repeat this process several times with different numbers of balloons. Children will get a bang out of this lesson!

Cathie Weaver
South Effingham Elementary School
Rincon, GA

Jennifer Bennett

POUNDS OF FUN!

If you've been pounding the pavement in search of activities to introduce your little ones to the concept of weight, search no further. Try these hands-on multidisciplinary activities for pounds of fun!

ideas by Betty Silkunas

My, How We've Grown!

Introduce the concept of weight with this "weigh-out" bulletin board. Label the back of a baby picture of each youngster with his name and birth weight. Staple the pictures atop construction paper squares before labeling each square with the featured child's birth weight. Display the labeled pictures on a bulletin board featuring the caption, "My, How We've Grown!" Pounds of fun are sure to follow as youngsters try to guess each baby's identity.

One Pound, Please

Bag a pound of jelly bean fun with this weighing activity. Place an empty plastic bag atop a diet scale. Have youngsters take turns counting as they add one jelly bean at a time to the bag. Continue adding jelly beans until the scale registers one pound. For a sweet treat, allow youngsters to feast on the entire pound of jelly beans.

One Pounders

Youngsters can get a feel for a pound with this activity. Help each youngster use a diet scale to weigh a pound of modeling clay. Then have him pound away and mold his clay into an original one-pound creation. Label each molded creation as shown; then display it with the other creations and additional items which weigh one pound.

What's Shakin'?

Youngsters will shake up pounds of excitement as they turn 16 ounces of cream into butter. Pour two ounces of very cold, heavy cream into each of eight baby food jars, then tightly secure the lids. Divide youngsters into pairs or small groups. Have the youngsters in each group take turns shaking the cream until butter forms. Pour off the buttermilk. Add salt to the butter if desired; then spread it atop crackers or muffins.

Mystery Pounds

Pound for pound, this estimation activity can't be beat! Fill each of a dozen paper lunch bags with different items such as pencils, cotton balls, pennies, or apples. Be sure that the contents of several of the bags weigh exactly one pound; then staple the bags closed. Display the mystery bags on a table. Have each child lift and shake each bag, attempting to identify its contents. Then ask a different volunteer to lift each bag, guess whether or not its contents weigh one pound, and weigh the bag to verify his guess. Reveal the contents of each bag, displaying the items which weigh exactly one pound.

Weighty Tug-of-War

In preparation for a class tug-of-war, weigh each child; then record his name and weight on a chart. Have each child use fabric paint to paint his name on the front of a T-shirt and his weight on the back of the shirt. After the paint has dried, have each youngster don his shirt. Divide youngsters into several teams; then have each team pull its weight in a series of tug-of-war contests.

Class Weigh-in

Use a calculator to total your youngsters' combined weight. Write the total on a large barbell cutout. Display the cutout along with the caption, "We Weigh As Much As…." Then, with the barbell cutout, display pictures of other objects which weigh approximately the same amount as the entire class.

Weight Lifters

Here's an activity youngsters can really put their weight into! Seal five pounds of sand in each of ten heavy-duty Ziploc® bags. In turn, have each youngster hold a sturdy laundry basket and count aloud by fives as you place bags of sand in the basket. Stop when he can hold no more, having the entire class count by fives as you remove the bags from the basket.

Sack Race

Sack races create pounds of hoppin' good fun! Place ten, five-pound bags of sand (see "Weight Lifters") in an empty, 50-pound, burlap potato sack. After a brief discussion of how potatoes are shipped, help each youngster attempt to lift the bag. For a gross-motor activity that's sure to have hearts pounding, have youngsters use additional burlap sacks to practice sack racing.

A Pound Of ABCs

As youngsters snack on samples of pound cake, challenge them to think of places where things are sold by the pound. Then have them name one item for each letter of the alphabet that can be purchased by the pound, as you list them on the chalkboard. Conclude your weighty discussion by having youngsters use a long length of bulletin-board paper to make a picture collage of items that are sold by the pound.

Kindergarten Math-In-A-Can

idea by Marla Hawthorne • Coshocton County Schools • Coshocton, OH

Strengthen the home/school bond by providing parents with a versatile and easy-to-use set of materials for home-based math reinforcement. Invite parents of kindergartners to school for an evening make-and-take session. Provide a kit of materials so that each student and his family can make the kindergartner's Math-In-A-Can center. Include in each kit the items listed (right). To assemble and use the Math-In-A-Can center, have parents follow the instructions in the note (below).

Each Math-In-A-Can Kit Should Include:

- an empty coffee can, preferably lidded
- one copy of the can wraps on page 27
- scissors
- crayons
- four, small self-adhesive Velcro circles (for attaching the can wraps to the can)
- ten one-inch ceramic tiles
- a permanent marker (optional)
- ten small pieces of magnetic tape
- a resealable plastic bag containing 12 lima beans that have been spray-painted on one side, making one side of each bean dark while the other remains light
- a resealable plastic bag
- a signed copy of the parent note below

Dear Parent,

Welcome to Math-In-A-Can. Math-In-A-Can is an easy-to-use learning center that can be used to reinforce many of the math skills your child is learning in school. Follow the instructions below to assemble and use the center.

To Assemble The Math-In-A-Can Center:

1. Cut out both can-wrap patterns.
2. Have your child color each of the can wraps.
3. Attach the loop halves of the Velcro® pieces to the back of each can-wrap strip, centering each piece opposite a dot on the front of the can-wrap strip.
4. Attach the hook halves of two Velcro® pieces to the can about 9 inches apart. This should position the Velcro® pieces so that they will hold each of the can wraps in place when each is wrapped around the can.
5. Using a permanent marker, write a numeral and draw a shape on each of the ten tile pieces to match the tiles shown on this letter.

6. Attach a small magnetic strip to the back of each tile.
7. Use the resealable bag to store an assortment of small items such as keys, thread spools, buttons, can tabs, and jug lids.
8. Check to make sure you have each of the following items inside your can to complete your Math-In-A-Can center: two can-wrap strips, ten labeled tiles with magnets, some lima beans in a bag, a bag of small items (like keys, thread spools, and buttons).

To Use Math-In-A-Can:

Activity A: Attach can-wrap A to the outside of the can. Have your child count each set of dots, name the number represented, and place the matching numeral tile on that set of dots.

Activity B: Without using the can or a can wrap, have the child place the tiles on a tabletop in random order. Ask the child to name each numeral.

Activity C: Without using the can or a can wrap, have the child place the tiles on a tabletop in random order. Ask the child to name each shape.

Activity D: Attach can-wrap B to the outside of the can. Have your child name each shape on the wrap and match each tile to its corresponding shape on the wrap.

Activity E: Using only the bag of small assorted items, have your child sort the contents by color, shape, size, purpose, etc.

Activity F: Use only the bag of lima beans for this pre-addition activity. Select a number from 1 to 12. Remove all but that many lima beans from the bag.

Tell your child that together you are going to find several combinations that add up to be the selected number. Have the child shake the bag and dump its contents. Ask your child to count the dark beans and the light beans. Verbalize this combination. (For example: "Three light beans and two dark beans equal five beans altogether.") Repeat this activity until several combinations have been identified for the specified number.

©The Education Center, Inc. • *The Best Of* THE MAILBOX® *Math • Preschool/Kindergarten • TEC1461*

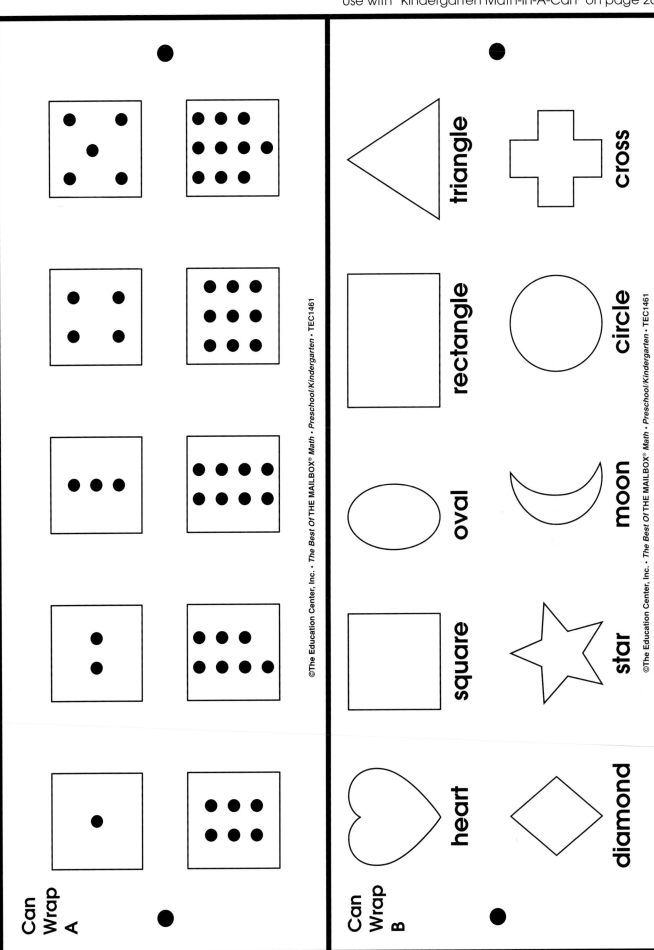

Can Wrap A

Can Wrap B

triangle

cross

rectangle

circle

oval

moon

square

star

heart

diamond

©The Education Center, Inc. • *The Best Of* THE MAILBOX® *Math* • *Preschool/Kindergarten* • TEC1461

©The Education Center, Inc. • *The Best Of* THE MAILBOX® *Math* • *Preschool/Kindergarten* • TEC1461

QUICK MATH FUN!

You can count on learning fun when you use these activities to teach and reinforce math concepts, such as one-to-one correspondence, counting, greater than, less than, addition, and subtraction.

Dots On A Die

One-to-one correspondence is sure to be mastered with a few rolls of this die. Make a large die by securely wrapping two square blocks in several layers of butcher paper. Use a marker to program the dots on the die. To do this activity, give each child six Hershey's® Kisses®. (You could use red-wrapped kisses near Valentine's Day, gold-wrapped kisses near St. Patrick's Day, etc.) Have a child roll the die, then place a kiss on each dot that is showing. Count the kisses on the dots as well as how many are left over. Of course—after each child has had several turns to roll the die—you just might have to sample some of the manipulatives!

Susan Burbridge—Preschool, All Saints Lutheran Preschool, Albuquerque, NM

Musical Chairs

Use the familiar game of Musical Chairs to help teach the concepts of *more* and *less*. Before you begin playing, tell youngsters that you will need one less chair than the number of students playing. (If you have students who use wheelchairs, adapt this game by using large sheets of laminated construction paper in place of the chairs. If necessary, you can adhere the sheets of paper to the floor with reusable adhesive.) After students have determined the number and arrangement of the chairs, begin playing in the traditional manner. After the first round of play, ask questions such as "How many children are left?", "Are there more children or chairs?", and "How many chairs do we need now?" Involve the children who are "out" by having them arrange the chairs, start/stop the music, and ask/answer the questions. Continue play until there is only one child left. Learning the concepts of *more* and *less* makes everyone a winner in this game!

Melissa Corrado—Gr. K, Kops For Kids, Totowa, NJ

Marshmallow Math

Sweeten your students' math skills with this marshmallow math activity. Give each child (or small group) a resealable plastic bag containing a desired number of colored marshmallows. (Pastel-colored marshmallows are often available in the spring.) Direct each child to sort his marshmallows according to color. Then have each child place his marshmallows on a graph. Help each child interpret what his graph reveals by asking questions such as "What color do you have the most of?", " What color do you have the least of?", and "How many more/less yellow ones do you have than green?" Afterwards serve some unhandled marshmallows for a sweet treat.

Gretchen Ranzinger–Gr. K, Conestoga Elementary School, Conestoga, PA

| PINK | YELLOW | GREEN | PURPLE |

Sunny-Day Shapes

A little fresh air and a few sticks of chalk can go a long way to reinforce shape recognition. On a nice sunny day, take your youngsters and a box or two of colored chalk to a surfaced section of your playground. Draw a large shape on the playground surface. Have children use chalk to trace that shape. Encourage youngsters to talk about the shape's characteristics as they work. Youngsters can also follow directions such as "Walk around the square," or "Jump inside the triangle." If your children are able, have them draw shapes independently. Then have each child move to a classmate's shape and trace that shape with another color of chalk.

Dawn Dumond—Grs. K-1, Mount View School, Thorndike, ME

Towers

To introduce and/or reinforce addition and subtraction concepts, engage your boys and girls in a game of Towers. Make a tower of a desired number of Unifix® cubes. Show youngsters your tower of ten cubes (for example). After children have counted the cubes in your tower, hide the tower behind your back and snap off or add on a number of cubes. Then show the tower to your students again. Ask them to figure out how many cubes were removed or added. Then give the tower to a child and have youngsters continue to play the game in the same manner until each child has had an opportunity to be the tower holder.

Susan Barr—Pre-1, Narragansett Elementary, Narragansett, RI

Stringy Fun

Your students will have yards of fun learning to work with nonstandard measurement. Give each child a designated length of string (such as 12 inches). Have youngsters use the strings to measure items in your school environment such as your classroom rug, a table, or the teacher's desk. Have children make estimates before they measure some of the objects, and compare the actual results. This is a great time to reinforce measurement vocabulary such as *long, short, wide,* and *narrow.*

Dawn Dumond—Grs. K-1

Beans!

This counting game will challenge your little ones to do some creative mathematical figuring. Program each section of an egg carton with a different numeral from 1–12. Provide a supply of beans (at least 78 for each carton in play) and two dice. To play the game, have a child roll one or two of the dice, count the dots showing, and place that many beans in the corresponding section of the egg carton. If a child rolls a number that has already been "beaned," he continues to roll the dice (or die) until he gets the exact number that he needs. If more than one child is playing the game, provide a programmed egg carton for each player and have children roll the dice in turn. In a group of players, if a child rolls a number that he has already beaned, he passes the dice to the next player and the game continues as before until all of the numerals have been beaned.

Susan Walder—Gr. K, Potomac Grade School, Potomac, IL

My
100 Stamp
Collection

by Beth Saunde

10 hearts

10 shamrocks

STAMP PAD

100th-Day Stamp Book

With this 100th-day booklet idea, there's a whole lotta' stampin' going on—and kids love it! For each child, staple together 11 half-sheets of construction paper. Have each child title and personalize his cover. Then provide a wide variety of rubber stamps and colorful stamp pads. Direct each child to stamp ten prints on each of his ten pages and label each page (or dictate for you to label them). After each child checks to be sure that he has ten pictures on each page, count together by tens until you reach the end of the book—and 100!

Pamela VanderBee—Gr. K, Townline School, Kentwood, MI

Popsicle® Math

Popsicle® sticks make great inexpensive manipulatives to help reinforce a variety of math skills. Give each child a designated number of Popsicle® sticks and a colorful sheet of construction paper to use as a work area. Ask each child to count his Popsicle® sticks. Then have him take away a given number of sticks. How many are left? Continue to add and subtract sticks as desired. As you add and subtract, you may even find a little creative artwork taking place!

Susan Burbridge—Preschool, All Saints Lutheran Preschool, Albuquerque, NM

The
Biggest
Big Book
Of
100

The Biggest Big Book Of 100

One hundred is quite a concept for little ones to grasp—and here's a huge way to help them do it! For each class or small group of children that will be participating in this project, prepare a big book page by cutting a full-size panel from a refrigerator box. Cover each page with bulletin-board paper. Then have each class or small group decorate a page with 100 things. For example, groups might choose to show 100 handprints, 100 lipstick kisses, or 100 kite cutouts. When all of the pages are complete, use one blade of a pair of scissors to poke holes in the edge of the pages. Bind the pages together with metal snap rings. After sharing this really big book with your class, be sure to leave it on display for further exploration.

Debbie Amason—Gr. K, West End Elementary, Milledgeville, GA

Transition Counting

Make smooth transitions and reinforce counting by using the catchy rhyme below. Stand or sit in a circle and say the rhyme together. When you reach the end, select a child to choose a number—12, for example. Count off 12 children and have the 12th child move to his next activity. Say the rhyme again and continue in the same manner until all students have been dismissed to their activities.

Bubble gum, bubble gum, in a dish.
How many pieces do you wish?

Donna Leonard—Preschool, Head Start, Dyersville, IA

What's The Magic Number?

Reinforce numeral recognition and more/less than concepts with this motivating game. Draw a number line—without numerals—on your chalkboard. Tell children that you are thinking of a magic number from 1–20 (for example) and you'd like them to figure out what that number is. As a child guesses a number, write it in the appropriate place on the number line. Then give students another clue, such as "The magic number is *more* than that." When additional guesses are announced, continue to write them on the number line and give additional clues related to the numerals showing. The thrill of accomplishment keeps youngsters asking for this game numerous times!

Kathy Curnow—Gr. K, Woolridge Elementary, Midlothian, VA

My
Coin
Book

by Alex Butner

Coin Books

Personalized coin books are fun to make and help make "cents" of coin recognition. For each coin that you wish to study, give each child a half-sheet of white copy paper. Have children make crayon rubbings of the head and tail sides of each coin, then write the name and value of the coin featured on that page. After each child has designed a cover page, staple all the pages together. Encourage youngsters to share their coin books with each other and with their family members.

Kaye Sowell—Gr. K, Pelahatchie Elementary, Pelahatchie, MS

Easy Money

Money is not an easy concept for little ones to grasp, but this interactive idea speeds the process right along! Try using commercial, overhead-projector money. The coins are large enough to enable youngsters to identify the likenesses and differences among the coins, and children just love to have a turn manipulating the coins on the screen.

Peggy Green—Gr. K, Bankston Elementary, Itta Bena, MS

Go Ahead—Spill The Beans!

In this activity, youngsters can spill the beans all they want! Spray-paint one side of a supply of white dried beans. When they are dry, place a handful of beans in each of several resealable plastic bags. To do this activity, have a child shake his bag of beans, then pour them out onto a flat surface. Depending on your youngsters' abilities, you can ask them questions such as "How many [blue] beans do you have?", "How many white beans?", and "How many beans altogether?" The beans can also be used for patterning or sorting activities. These are great math activities to extend a reading of *Jack And The Beanstalk*.

Lisa Haught—Gr. K, Arlington Elementary, Arlington, OH

Math Mix-Up

This activity provides lots of opportunities for numeral sequencing as well as numeral writing. Have each child tear a piece of paper into ten pieces (adapt this number as desired). Have each child count to be sure that he has ten pieces; then direct him to write a different numeral from 1–10 on each piece. Next have each child arrange the numbered pieces in numerical order. Store each child's pieces in a different resealable plastic bag. When you need a five-minute filler or a math warm-up activity, have each child select a bag, shake up the pieces, and place them in numerical order.

Cynthia Shutter—Gr. K, Highland-Biltmore, Portsmouth, VA

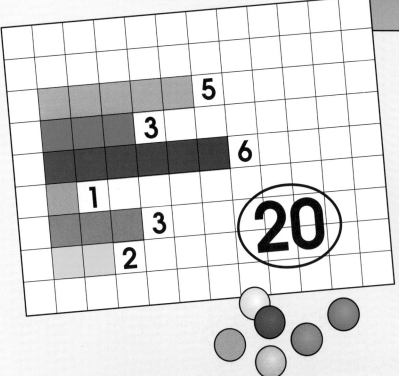

M&M's® Graphing

You won't have any trouble persuading youngsters to participate in this counting/graphing activity! Give each child a sheet of graph paper (approximately one-inch squares) and a snack-size bag of M&M's®. Have each child graph his candies by color on his graph paper. Then, using a corresponding crayon color, have him color one square for each candy of that color. Encourage each child to write the total number of each color on his graph. Then challenge each child to add the total number of candies. What could be more motivating than your very own stash of M&M's®?

Candi DeFran—Gr. K, East River Elementary, Grosse Ile, MI

People Pattern Person

Patterning can get rather creative when you use People Pattern Persons. Each day when you're ready to gather in your meeting area, choose a person to seat her classmates according to a pattern of her choice. She may, for example, seat her classmates in a boy, boy, girl pattern or in a pattern according to the color of clothing each child is wearing. When everyone has been seated, have children guess what pattern the People Pattern Person has created. Afterwards clap and snap the pattern for added reinforcement and fun.

Barbara Kitzen—Gr. K, Woodward Parkway Elementary, Farmingdale, NY

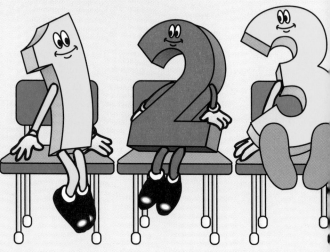

Beach Ball!

Involve those large-motor muscles in this easily adaptable math activity. Use a permanent marker to write a different numeral on each section of an inflated beach ball. Toss the ball to a child. When she catches the ball, have her hold the ball without moving her hands and determine which two numerals are nearest her hands. Use those two numerals as the basis for her specific activities. For example, you might ask that child to name the two numerals, write them on the chalkboard, count out that many manipulatives, decide which number is greater, or add the two numbers together. Next have that child toss the ball to a classmate. Continue in the same manner until each child has had at least one turn to catch and toss the ball. What a blast!

Lynn Wharton—Gr. K, Baker Elementary, Mobile, AL

A Lengthy Estimation

Stretch the minds and imaginations of your little ones as they practice making estimates. Place all of your Unifix® cubes on the floor of a long hallway, the gym, or your playground. Encourage each child to estimate how far the cubes will go if you put all of them together in one line. Have each child place a sticky note at the point of his prediction. If desired, also have youngsters predict how many cubes there are altogether.

Then begin the discovery process by having each child make lines containing ten cubes of one color. (Provide a ten-cube model for self-checking.) Attach the ten-cube lines together until all of the cubes are used. Have children compare their length predictions to the actual result. Then count by tens to see how many cubes there are altogether.

Wilma Droegemueller—Preschool/K, Zion Lutheran School, Mt. Pulaski, IL

Take A Guess!

Continue working on estimating skills with this ongoing activity. You will need a clear plastic jar with a lid and a copy of a note similar to the one shown. Choose a student to take the jar home and fill it with items such as those suggested in the note. When the jar is brought back to school, give each child an opportunity to estimate how many things are in the jar. If desired, write all of the guesses on the board and circle the highest and the lowest guesses. Then count the items in the jar. If there are many items to count, have youngsters count out groups of ten into paper cups. After discussing the results, select another child to take the jar home, and continue in the same manner.

Kelly A. Wong, Berlyn School, Ontario, CA

Estimation Jar
It is your child's turn to fill our estimation jar with items for us to count. We like to count items such as macaroni, peanuts, dried beans, buttons, etc.
Please return the jar tomorrow.
Thank you!

Ms. Wong

Rock Around The Clock

Watch time fly right by when you use this collection of learning activities to introduce your little clock-watchers to the concepts of time.

by Lucia Kemp Henry

Day Or Night? You're Right!

Inspire a timely, child-decorated bulletin board by simply discussing the concepts of day and night. To prepare the board, enlarge, color, and cut out the illustrations from the booklet cover on page 37. Mount the girl and daytime window cutout on one side of the board and the boy and nighttime window cutout on the other side of the board. Visually divide the board in half with a long strip of construction paper; then label the halves with "Day" and "Night" respectively. Brainstorm a list of activities in which your youngsters are involved on a regular basis. Have each child choose an activity from the list to illustrate, then write (or dictate) whether that activity takes place during the day or night. Have each youngster mount his finished picture on the appropriate side of the board.

Wee Watches

Enhance time-recognition skills by providing each youngster with a 'round-the-clock model of his own. To make a play watch, poke two small holes on opposite sides of the flat part of a snap-on milk jug lid. In order to enlarge the holes a bit, snip away the extra plastic with a pair of sharp scissors. Thread a six-inch length of 1/4-inch-wide elastic through the holes, overlapping the ends about 3/4 inch. Staple the elastic ends together; then pull the elastic down so that the stapled ends lie flat on the inside of the lid. Duplicate the watch face pattern on page 44 onto tagboard; then cut it out. Glue the watch face to the inside ridge of the lid, concealing the stapled ends of the elastic. When the glue is dry, a youngster may wear his watch with the smooth side of the lid resting against his wrist.

Clockworks

Nothing facilitates learning more than hands-on experience! Help youngsters learn numeral sequencing as it relates to a clock face by providing a manipulative clock puzzle for each child. To make a clock puzzle, duplicate the clock pattern on page 43 onto tagboard. Have each child write her name on the base of her clock, then color the rest of the clock. Glue the clock picture to the front of a string-tie envelope. Laminate the envelope if desired. Provide a laminated tagboard copy of the numeral patterns on page 44. (Depending on your youngsters' skill levels, you might ask an adult volunteer to cut out the numeral patterns along the bold outlines.) Have each child cut apart her numeral patterns on the dotted lines. Store these puzzle pieces in the string-tie envelope. For reference, have each youngster wear her play watch (from "Wee Watches") while working on her clock puzzle.

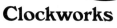

Ticktock, ticktock.
Put the numbers on the clock.

Katrina

What Time Is It?

Here's a hands-on booklet that will allow little ones to freely explore the relationships between the big hand, the little hand, and the numerals on a clock. To make a booklet, duplicate the cover and booklet pages 1–4 (pages 37–41) onto construction paper. Cut along the dotted-clock outlines on the cover and booklet pages 1–4. Duplicate booklet page 5 onto tagboard. Trim all of the booklet pages around the heavy black outline. Cut a big and little clock hand from tagboard scraps; then use a brad to attach them to the middle of the clock on page 5. Sequence the booklet pages; then staple all of the booklet pages together along the left margin. Provide lots of time for free exploration. To use the book formally, have each child position the hands on his clock to match the small clock illustration on each page. Then discuss what the children are doing on each page and the time of day that is represented.

Ticktock Says The Clock

Make your own flannelboard characters from the booklet illustrations (pages 37–42) to accompany each verse of the poem below. Duplicate the characters from the booklet onto construction paper; then color (or have youngsters color) the characters and cut them out. Laminate each of the characters before backing them with pieces of felt or Velcro®. As you read or recite the poem below, have each youngster take a turn putting the characters on the board at just the right time!

Ticktock says the clock,
Telling time each day.
Telling us to wake and sleep,
And when to work and play.

Ticktock says the clock.
Now it's time to rise.
I get up at seven o'clock
And rub my sleepy eyes.

Ticktock says the clock.
Now it's time to run.
School begins at nine o'clock.
Learning's lots of fun!

Ticktock says the clock.
Now it's time for lunch.
I sit down at twelve o'clock
And then I munch and crunch.

Ticktock says the clock.
Now it's time to play.
I have fun at four o'clock—
My favorite time of day!

Ticktock says the clock.
Now it's time for bed.
I lie down at eight o'clock
And rest my sleepy head.

by Lucia Kemp Henry

8:00 Arrive at school.

8:30 Circle time

9:00 Centers

10:00 Play outside.

School Day Timeline

Create a school day timeline with your youngsters to visually represent the activities for each hour of the school day. Brainstorm a list of activities in which your youngsters are involved during the course of a typical school day. Organize the ideas by hour (or half hour if necessary). Program a large sheet of construction paper for each activity by writing the name of the activity and the time at which it takes place at the bottom of the paper. Have youngsters illustrate each of the activities. Display the illustrated activities in chronological order on a wall. For a fun challenge, have your little time-tellers sequence the activities independently.

Clock Cards

Provide this matching game in a learning center to aid little ones in their new time-telling tasks. Duplicate the time cards on page 44 onto tagboard. Laminate the cards; then cut them out. Next remove pages 45–47; then cut out the clock cards. Store the time cards and the clock cards in a zippered plastic bag. To play, have a youngster match each written time to a clock showing the same time.

Vary the use of the clock cards by having a youngster sequence the cards by the hour indicated on each of the clock faces or by having a small group of youngsters play a Concentration game. To play a Concentration game, place all of the clock cards and time cards facedown on the floor or a table. In turn, have each youngster turn over a time card and a clock card. If the two times match, the youngster keeps the pair and takes another turn. If the times do not match, the cards are returned to the facedown position, and play continues with the next player. The object of the game is to accumulate as many pairs as possible. It's also fun to play Match-In-A-Minute. Use the same directions as in the Concentration game, but include a time crunch. The object of this game is to see how many matches a team of children (taking turns) can make in a minute.

Time To Sing

Sing away the hours with this familiar, snappy tune. Display a clock with movable hands (such as a Judy clock). Whisper a time to a selected child; then have him set the clock to the time given. Lead the entire class in singing the song below, allowing youngsters to fill in the appropriate time in the last line of the song. To include morning, afternoon, and night concepts, describe the time of day before you begin singing. For example, if you have a child set a clock for eight o'clock and you'd like to indicate that it is eight o'clock at night, you might say, "This is the time when it's dark outside and we're getting ready for bed." Then begin singing the song.

The Time
(sung to the tune of "The Muffin Man")

Oh, do you know what time it is,
What time it is, what time it is?
Oh, do you know what time it is?
It's *[supply the number]* o'clock in the *[morning, afternoon, or night]*.

adapted from an idea by LeAnn Peterson—Gr. K, Grosse Pointe Woods, MI

Cookie Clocks

Wind up your clock activities with these confectionery delights. To make a cookie clock, cut a large circle from your favorite rolled sugar-cookie dough; then place it on a cookie sheet. Press candies into the cookie to represent the numerals on a clock. (If you're aiming for accurate placement of the candies, try positioning the candies in the 12 o'clock, 3 o'clock, 6 o'clock, and 9 o'clock positions first.) Bake the cookie as directed. When the cookie is cool, pipe clock hands onto the cookie with decorator's frosting in a tube. To make *movable* clock hands, squirt a dollop of frosting only in the center of the cookie; then press one end of each of two lengths of licorice into the frosting. When a youngster wishes to "change the time," have him take the licorice ends out of the frosting, adjust the clock hands, then resecure the licorice ends in the frosting. Mmm—what time do you have?

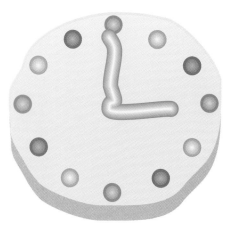

"Time-ly" Reading

Clocks And More Clocks
by Pat Hutchins
Published by Aladdin Paperbacks

The Grouchy Ladybug
by Eric Carle
Published by HarperCollins Children's Books

My First Book Of Time
by Claire Llewellyn
Published by Dorling Kindersley Publishing, Inc.

What Time Is It?

by

Note To Teacher: Use with "Day Or Night? You're Right!" on page 34 and "What Time Is It?" on page 34 and "Ticktock Says The Clock" on page 35.

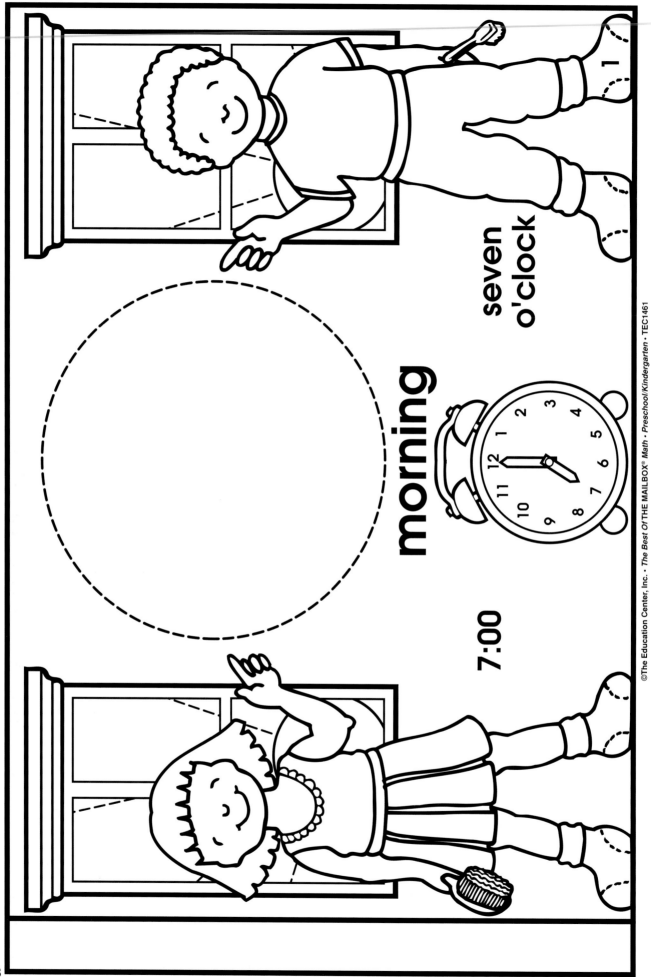

morning

seven
o'clock

7:00

38

Note To Teacher: Use with "What Time Is It?" and "Ticktock Says The Clock" on page 35.

schooltime

9:00

nine o'clock

Note To Teacher: Use with "What Time Is It?" and "Ticktock Says The Clock" on page 35.

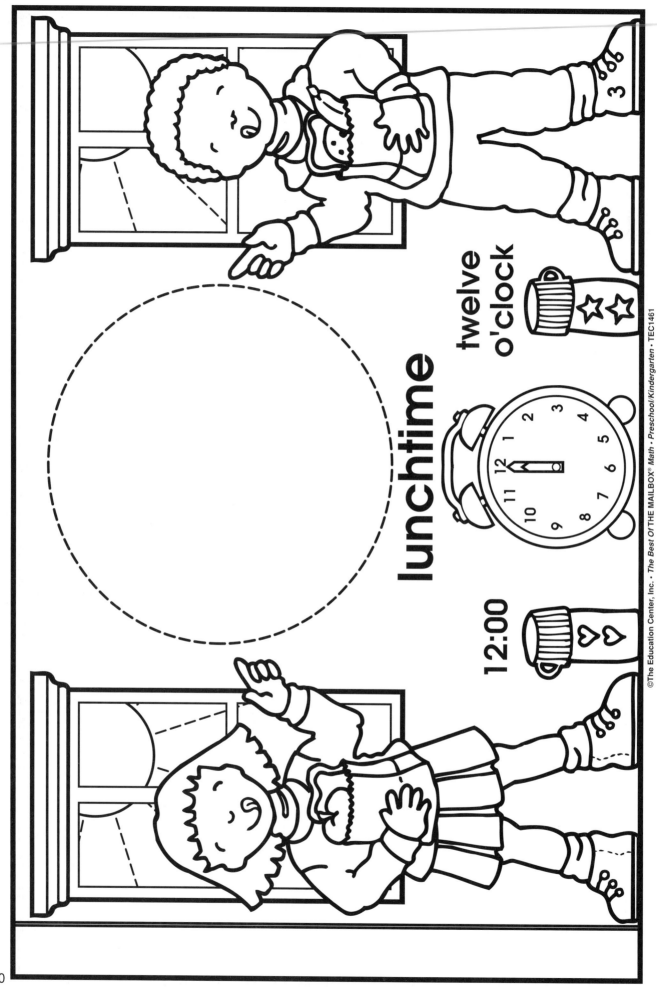

lunchtime

twelve o'clock

12:00

©The Education Center, Inc. • *The Best Of THE MAILBOX® Math* • *Preschool/Kindergarten* • TEC1461

Note To Teacher: Use with "What Time Is It?" and "Ticktock Says The Clock" on page 35.

40

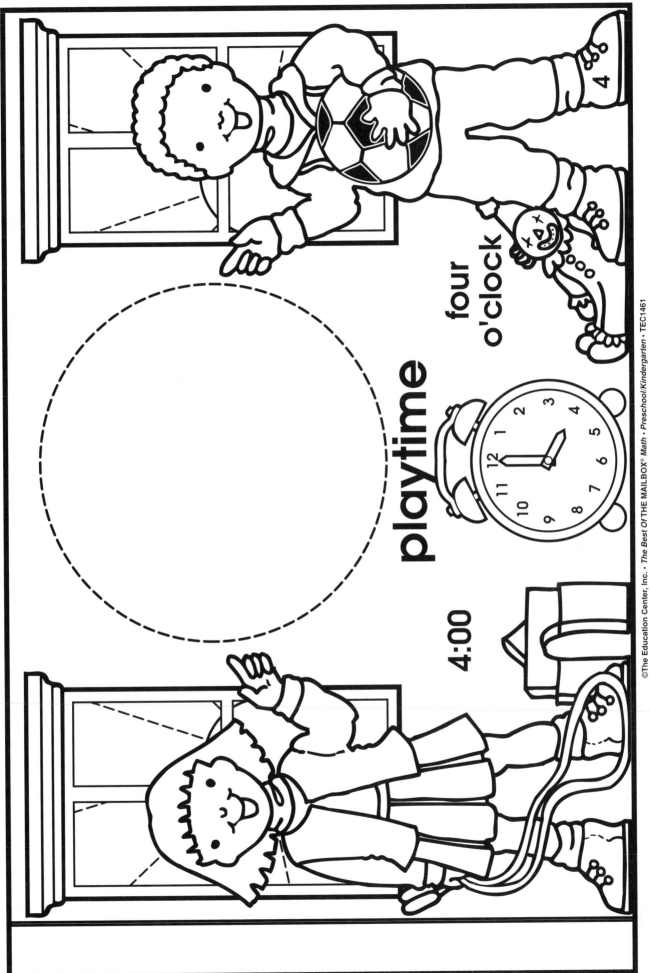

playtime

four o'clock

4:00

Note To Teacher: Use with "What Time Is It?" and "Ticktock Says The Clock" on page 35.

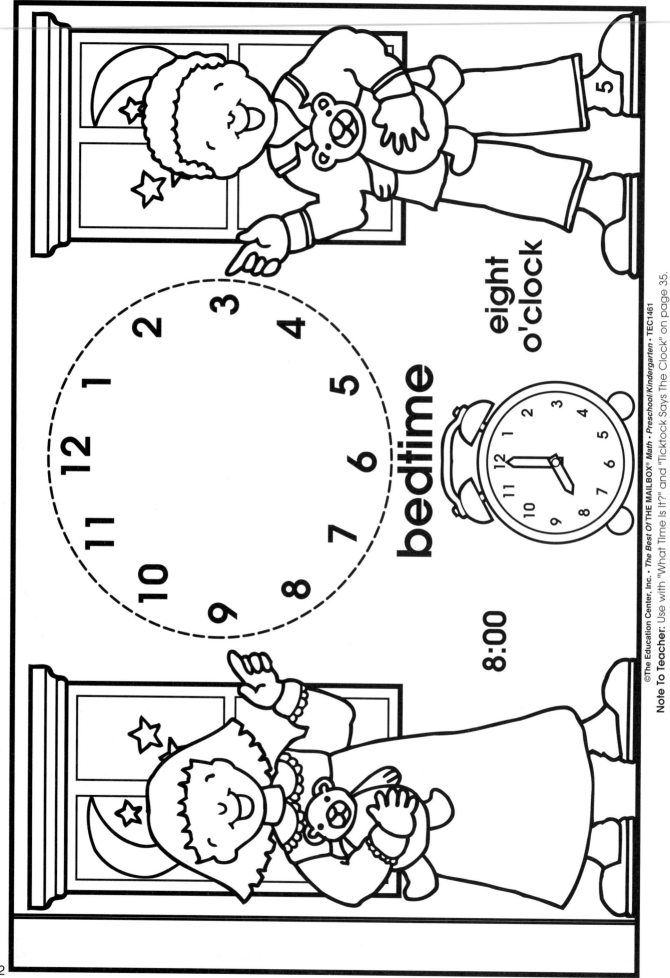

bedtime

eight o'clock

8:00

42

©The Education Center, Inc. • *The Best Of THE MAILBOX® Math* • *Preschool/Kindergarten* • TEC1461

Note To Teacher: Use with "What Time Is It?" and "Ticktock Says The Clock" on page 35.

Ticktock, ticktock.

Put the numbers on the clock.

Patterns
Use with "Clockworks"
on page 34.

Watch Face Pattern
Use with "Wee Watches"
on page 34.

Patterns
Time Cards

Use with "Clock Cards"
on page 36.

1:00	2:00	3:00	4:00
5:00	6:00	7:00	8:00
9:00	10:00	11:00	12:00

©The Education Center, Inc.

©The Education Center, Inc.

©The Education Center, Inc.

©The Education Center, Inc.

©The Education Center, Inc.

©The Education Center, Inc.

©The Education Center, Inc.

©The Education Center, Inc.

©The Education Center, Inc.

©The Education Center, Inc.

©The Education Center, Inc.

©The Education Center, Inc.

Math & Literature

Moja Means One:
Swahili Counting Book
Written by Muriel Feelings • Illustrated by Tom Feelings
Published by Dial Books for Young Readers

Open this book to teach youngsters to count to ten in Swahili, an African language, and to learn about East African culture. The same wife/husband team created the companion to this book, Jambo Means Hello: Swahili Alphabet Book.

Learning a new language can be fascinating. Read the book aloud; then have youngsters repeat after you as you count to ten in Swahili. Help youngsters locate Africa on a globe. Invite guest speakers into your class to teach your youngsters more about African culture and language. Or take your youngsters to see an African museum exhibit.

As is the tradition in African villages, gather your youngsters in a darkened area and share traditional African tales. Some excellent books to read are *Why Mosquitoes Buzz In People's Ears: A West African Tale* by Verna Aardema, *Anansi The Spider: A Tale From The Ashanti* adapted by Gerald McDermott, *How The Guinea Fowl Got Her Spots: A Swahili Tale Of Friendship* retold by Barbara Knutson, and *Rabbit Makes A Monkey Of Lion: A Swahili Tale* retold by Verna Aardema.

When Sheep Cannot Sleep:
The Counting Book
Written & Illustrated by Satoshi Kitamura
Published by Farrar, Straus & Giroux, Inc.

What do you do when you can't sleep? Count sheep, of course! But what does a sleepless sheep count? Youngsters will get a kick out of accompanying Woolly, the sheep with insomnia, on a late-night "count-capade."

Just before Woolly falls off to sleep, he imagines all his relatives and friends. Since there are so many, counting them is great practice. Youngsters can make a herd of sheep for their own counting practice. Trace the shape of one of each youngster's hands onto construction paper. Assist each youngster as he cuts out his hand outline, glues cotton batting to the palm area, and colors a nose, an eye, and an ear. Display all of these sheep together and count them in unison.

There's another late-night counting book with a rural setting that has a decidedly different look. Read aloud *The Midnight Farm* by Reeve Lindbergh. After reading it and *When Sheep Cannot Sleep,* ask youngsters which book they prefer and why. Then have each youngster add a sqaure to a graph to show which nighttime counting book he prefers.

Anno's Counting Book
Written & Illustrated by Mitsumasa Anno
Published by HarperCollins Children's Books

Get back to basics with this wordless book that illustrates numbers by documenting the growth of a village. Your youngsters will have fun counting the growing numbers of houses, trees, people, and animals on each page and using cubes to show one-to-one correspondence.

At the back of the book, Mr. Anno notes that peple began counting in order to keep track of things in their daily lives. He mentions that early people used counters to keep track of things. Introduce youngsters to this concept by having them use cubes, counters, or pebbles to represent things around them. For example, have each youngster use his manipulatives to make a set equal to the number of chalkboard erasers you have. Then encourage each youngster to use cubes in his spare time to show a set equal to each cube set in the book.

Cover a bulletin board with green paper hills and a light blue paper sky. Have each child color the four patterns on a construction-paper copy of page 52. After each youngster cuts out his patterns, attach several cutouts to the bulletin board. Make a rebus question strip for each set of objects and attach it to the board. For example: "How many [picture of a tree]s?" Supply number cards. Have youngsters take turns counting and pinning the correct number card by each question. Regularly remove or add pictures to vary the counting challenge.

The Right Number Of Elephants
Written by Jeff Sheppard • Illustrated by Felicia Bond
Published by HarperCollins Children's Books

This silly story uses specific numbers of elephants to help a child get through some very silly situations. The illustrations will challenge students to count the elephants correctly.

Use the elephant pattern on page 52 to make counting cards that emphasize one-to-one correspondence. Reproduce, color, cut out, and glue varying numbers of elephants to tagboard cards. Supply your youngsters with a container of peanuts to match to each set of elephants, giving each elephant one peanut.

Use this silly story as the inspiration for creative writing and counting. Have each child name a task or chore and decide how many elephants it takes to complete the task. Have each youngster dictate a sentence describing how many elephants it takes to do the chore. Write the sentence at the bottom of a piece of paper. Encourage each youngster to illustrate his story humorously.

Pattern

Use with *The Right Number Of Elephants* on page 51.

Patterns

Use with *Anno's Counting Book* on page 51.

Ten, Nine, Eight

Written & Illustrated by Molly Bang
Published by William Morrow & Company, Inc.

This book features a simple, but effective, countdown to bedtime.

This activity, which focuses on counting backwards, is an effective follow-up to a reading of *Ten, Nine, Eight.* Have the students work collectively with you or in separate small groups to write and illustrate a book with the same story pattern as *Ten, Nine, Eight.* Before students begin, brainstorm environments that they may want to feature. Some choices, for example, are the playground, the classroom, and the beach. Each book will be uniquely different.

Lisa Kranz—Gr. K • St. Ann School • Lansing, IL

The Button Box

Written by Margarette S. Reid
Illustrated by Sarah Chamberlain
Published by Dutton Children's Books

Examining the contents of a button box can be a fascinating pastime. The child in the story sorts the buttons into several classifications and talks about what some buttons are made of.

Use *The Button Box* as a springboard for any number of math activities. To begin, have students comment on the illustrations in the book, making generalizations about ways to classify the objects. Or have one student ask another student a question related to the number or colors in a given set of objects. Later place the book in a center with an assortment of buttons, bottle caps, or beads. Encourage students to sort the objects by size, color, and shape.

Joanne Schlegel—Gr. K • Manito School • Oakland, NJ

What Comes In 2's, 3's, & 4's?

Written by Suzanne Aker
Illustrated by Bernie Karlin
Published by Simon & Schuster Children's Books

Numeration has meaningful beginnings in this book. As it so simply points out, arms and wings are things that usually come in twos. But traffic signal lights come in threes and wheels often come in fours.

After sharing *What Comes In 2's, 3's, & 4's?* with your youngsters, ask them to brainstrom things that come in twos, threes, and fours—other than those mentioned in the book. Encourage students to think of elements in different school situations to help them with their brainstorming efforts. Have each student create a small booklet that contains related pictures. When they take their booklets home, ask students to continue their search for twos, threes, and fours at home.

Carmen C. Carpenter—Pre/K • MacGregor Creative School Knightdale, NC

Walt Disney's One Hundred One Dalmations: A Counting Book

Written by Fran Manushkin
Illustrated by Russell Hicks
Published by Disney Press

If your youngsters are enthusiastic fans of the movie or video version of Walt Disney's One Hundred One Dalmations, *they'll enjoy the counting book, too.*

After sharing *Walt Disney's One Hundred One Dalmations: A Counting Book* with your youngsters, ask each child to draw, color, and cut out several dalmation pups. Explain that you will need 99 pups altogether. Display all 99 pups around the room in sets of ten, if desired. Also display two adult dalmatian cutouts to be the proud parents. When students have some free time, encourage them to count the pups and the adults to confirm that all 101 are there!

Catherine L. Pesa—Preschool Hearing Impaired
Paul C. Bunn • Youngstown, OH

The Doorbell Rang
Written & Illustrated by Pat Hutchins
Published by Greenwillow Books

When twelve yummy cookies were taken from the oven, Sam and Victoria decided to split the batch equally, so they had six each. But a couple of neighbors dropped in, making it necessary to split the batch four ways, so each child had three cookies. Predictably the doorbell continued to ring, causing the youngsters to reallocate the cookies a couple more times.

After reading *The Doorbell Rang,* have students enact the story using a dozen chocolate-chip cookie cutouts. Assign parts, and reread the story. Each time the doorbell rings in the story, have more students enter from offstage. Designate a different child to divide the cookies equally among the students, each time students are added to the group. Repeat the enactment, if necessary, to give each child an opportunity to participate. Afterwards, have students prepare a real batch of cookies and divide them equally, or divide the contents of a box of Cookie-Crisp®.

Mary Sutula—Preschool • Orlando, FL
Kelly A. Wong • Berlyn School • Ontario, CA

Once your youngsters have enacted *The Doorbell Rang,* they will take delight in a learning center based on the same theme. Make 24 chocolate-chip cookie cutouts and attach a strip of magnetic tape to the back of each. Place the cutouts on a metal cookie sheet and put it in a center along with small paper plates and a plastic spatula. To use the center in pairs or small groups, have children take turns serving equal portions of cookies to the participants. Encourage youngsters to vary the number of cookie cutouts that are originally on the cookie sheet. They could start with 10 or 12 cookies (rather than 24), for example.

Jean Wark—Gr. K • Perkins Elementary • St. Petersburg, FL

Ten Apples Up On Top!
Written by Theo. LeSieg
Illustrated by Roy McKie
Published by Random House, Inc.

In this story, three zany characters parade around with various numbers of apples on their heads. Due to an unfortunate turn of events, an entire load of apples overturns with delightful results.

For a tasty touch, supply each youngster with an apple or apple wedge before reading *Ten Apples Up On Top!* aloud. Then ask each child to draw and color an illustration of a dog at the bottom of a sheet of construction paper. Provide an apple-shaped rubber stamp and a red stamp pad, and encourage each student to stamp ten apples on his dog's head. Extend the activity, if desired, by having each youngster draw another animal and embellish him with more (or fewer) apples than the original one has. Or encourage students to add characters and apples to illustrate a number sequence or to illustrate a pattern.

Lori J. Brown—Preschool • Lebanon Valley Brethren Home
Palmyra, PA

After reading aloud *Ten Apples Up On Top!,* have each student select red, green, or yellow paper and cut an apple shape from it. On a labeled graph, have each child temporarily attach his apple cutout according to color. Discuss the results of the graph with your students. Then have students work cooperatively to draw and color animal characters. Or trace and cut out the whole-body outlines of a few student volunteers, and have the students work in small groups to add details to resemble the students who posed for the tracings. Once the student-decorated designs are complete, mount them on a bulletin board or in a hallway. Have students use the apples from the graph and additional apple cutouts to tape ten apples on each character's head.

Kathleen McCarthy—Gr. K • Frankfurt Elementary School
Frankfurt, Germany
Katie Bailey—Gr. K • Edgewood School • Bristol, CT

Ten Black Dots

Written & Illustrated by Donald Crews
Published by Greenwillow Books

What can you imagine a simple dot to be? In this book, a dot becomes everything from a snowman's nose to a moon. Each time the transformation occurs, there's a different set of dot objects, providing an additional opportunity for counting.

After reading *Ten Black Dots* to your students, ask them to imagine other things that the black dots could have represented. Brainstorm with your students for a while; then give each student a sheet of construction paper, a set of ten precut construction-paper dots, and miscellaneous art supplies. Encourage each student to use the provided materials to imaginatively incorporate any number of his dots into an original picture. Afterwards, as each student dictates, write his description of his artwork. Display each picture with its description.

Sandra Patane—Preschool
Fulton ABC Preschool
Fulton, NY

My dog Spot

Here's another interesting follow-up activity for *Ten Black Dots* that promotes creativity as well as counting. Have each youngster press the eraser end of a new pencil onto a black stamp pad; then have him print ten dots randomly on a sheet of paper, reinking the eraser as necessary. When the printed dots have dried, have the student imagine how the dots could be connected to make a design. Encourage each student to connect his dots with crayon or pencil, then color the resulting design.

Sandra Patane—Preschool

Ten In A Bed

Written & Illustrated by Mary Rees
(This book is out of print. Check your library.)

An old familiar tune is put into the context of a contemporary sleepover in this wonderfully illustrated book. Youngsters are repeatedly ousted from the bed which originally held ten friends, so there are many opportunities to lay the groundwork for subtraction studies.

Once you've read aloud *Ten In A Bed,* ask for volunteers to act out the story line. Have two adults or older students hold the sides of a blanket or sheet at a height that allows the audience to see the faces of students who stand behind it. Ask for ten volunteers to stand behind the sheet or blanket. Then, as you read the story, have youngsters exit in turn to the audience's right. When there is one child remaining behind the sheet or blanket, vary the words of the story by saying, "Alone at last!" Repeat the activity until each child has had an oppportunity to participate. During the story repetitions, pause occasionally to ask the audience to verbalize how many students were behind the covers, how many are left, and how many remain.

Mary Bol—Preschool • Jenison Christian Preschool
Jenison, MI

Seven Little Rabbits

Written by John Becker
Illustrated by Barbara Cooney
Published by Walker And Company

Seven little rabbits set out to see their old friend toad. One-by-one along the way they succumb to fatigue and stop to rest at a mole's place. Consequently this book makes an interesting starting point for number-related activities.

Have seven students wear rabbit-ear headbands that have been numbered *one* through *seven*. Ask them to stand in order by number where they can easily be seen. Have the remaining students observe the seven rabbits; then ask the audience members to hide their eyes. Meanwhile silently instruct one of the rabbits to turn away from the audience. Instruct the students in the audience to look up and tell the numeral of the bunny that is turned away. Have the bunny again turn to face the audience so that they can check their answers. Ask one or more of the audience members who gave the correct response to take the place of a student who is standing. To start the cycle again, have the students in the audience hide their eyes and select another student to turn away from the class. Continue playing as before until each student has had a turn to be a rabbit.

Carolyn Meadows—Gr. K • West Hills Elementary
Knoxville, TN

The Grouchy Ladybug

Written & Illustrated by Eric Carle
Published by HarperCollins Children's Books

As a grouchy ladybug is learning a lesson on inter-personal skills, your little ones can learn timely lessons too. In trying to pick a fight, the ladybug challenges a different creature each hour—giving you the perfect opening for time discussions.

Read aloud *The Grouchy Ladybug* to ease into a discussion on time. Depending on the ability levels of your students, discuss the clock face; lengths of time such as the second, minute, and hour; increments of time that are marked on the clock face; or specific times that students can identify. If possible remove your classroom clock from the wall or obtain a suitable substitute. Use the clock to demonstrate the concepts that you discuss with youngsters. Also have students use a clock to match each of several times displayed in *The Grouchy Ladybug*. Before you replace your wall clock, attach a ladybug cutout to it, as a reminder to students that they've encountered *The Grouchy Ladybug*.

Ann M. Gudowski—Preschool • St. George's Academy
Laguna Hills, CA

Once you've read *The Grouchy Ladybug* to your youngsters, they'll know just what that ill-mannered insect was doing at each hour on the hour. But are they aware of what they are doing each hour? Prepare for this activity in advance by using a clock stamp and stamp pad or clock faces cut from workbooks to label an open chart for each hour of the school day. Then set a timer so that you'll remember to pause on the next hour. When the timer goes off, have a student volunteer dictate something about what the class was involved in when the timer sounded. Write his comments on an index card and attach it to the chart. At the end of the day, review what students were doing on the hour throughout the school day. To repeat the exercise at another time, just remove the cards, and have students fill in and attach new ones.

Kaye Sowell—Gr. K • Pelahatchie Elementary
Pelahatchie, MS

26 Letters And 99 Cents

Written & Illustrated by Tana Hoban
Published by Greenwillow Books

Tana Hoban turned two irresistible books topsy-turvy beneath one set of covers. The "99 Cents" part of the book, which features photographs of groups of coins, can be used to effectively stimulate a variety of coin-related discussions and activities.

After sharing *26 Letters And 99 Cents* with your students, place it in a center with a generous supply of real or imitation coins. Encourage students to visit the center individually or in pairs. To use the center, have the students open the "99 Cents" portion of the book and place matching coins atop each coin photograph. One of the bonuses of this activity may be that students will more closely observe the design elements on both sides of each coin used.

Betty Ann Silkunas • Lansdale, PA

Alexander, Who Used To Be Rich Last Sunday

Written & Illustrated by Judith Viorst
Published by Simon & Schuster Children's Division

If you're looking for a good way to end a unit on money, read aloud Alexander, Who Used To Be Rich Last Sunday. *In this lively book, a boy neglects to save money.*

Read aloud *Alexander, Who Used To Be Rich Last Sunday*. Then discuss with your students why it is important to save money. Have the youngsters make piggy banks to help them with their money-saving efforts. To make a piggy bank, begin by painting a toilet-tissue roll and two 2-inch poster-board circles with pink paint. When the circles have dried, cut an opening in one of them through which a quarter can pass. Tape a short, curled, curling-ribbon length to the other circle. Decorate the roll to resemble the features of a pig's face. Glue the circles to the ends of the roll. Now that everyone has his own piggy bank, there's no reason your youngsters can't begin saving!

Zena Weeks—Gr. K • Cypress Creek Elementary
Ruskin, FL

Inch By Inch

Written & Illustrated by Leo Lionni
Published by HarperCollins Children's Books

An inchworm, who's in danger of being gobbled up by a robin, convinces the bird to spare his life because he has the marvelous talent of being able to measure things.

You'll have little trouble coaxing your youngsters into measuring when you use this activity. Show students a jar of fruit-flavored candy worms prior to reading aloud *Inch By Inch*. Encourage students to estimate the number of worms that are in the jar. Remove the worms one at a time as students count them. Having piqued their interest, read aloud *Inch By Inch*. Afterward, give each student a candy worm and challenge him to determine its length in inches and centimeters. Also have each student locate and name items that are shorter than (and longer than) their candy worms. Before concluding this wormy topic, have each student color a space on a blank grid to graph the colors of the worms. Encourage students to interpret the results. Since the worms used for this activity are sure to be well-handled, provide a separate jar of candy worms for snacking.

Melana Watley • Britt David Elementary • Columbus, GA

 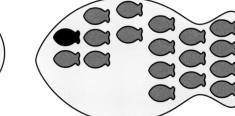

Swimmy

Written & Illustrated by Leo Lionni
Published by Alfred A. Knopf Books For Young Readers

In this beloved tale, small red fish and a tiny black fish cooperate to make themselves appear to be one giant fish. Reel your youngsters in for some fun in a related fish-counting game.

Begin making this follow-up game for *Swimmy* by cutting out lots of small red fish shapes and one black fish shape. Arrange the fish on poster board to resemble the shape of a large fish. Trace the configuration of the large fish shape onto the poster board. Remove the small fish, and store them in a fishbowl. Cut along the large fish outline. Place the large fish shape, the bowl of red fish, the black fish, and a numbered spinner in a center. To use the center, youngsters in a small group take turns spinning the spinner. After reading the number on each spin, the player takes a matching number of fish from the bowl and places them within the large fish outline. The student who takes the last red fish from the bowl may also place Swimmy, the black fish, in the correct location to be the large fish's eye. At that point, everyone wins!

Jill Berrner—Gr. K • Laurel Elementary • Brea, CA

If You Give A Mouse A Cookie

Written by Laura Joffe Numeroff
Illustrated by Felicia Bond
Published by HarperCollins Children's Books

What if you gave a mouse a cookie? What would happen next? Well, as you can see in this book, there's no stopping the whims of a mouse, once you've indulged him.

Read aloud *If You Give A Mouse A Cookie;* then use the story line as springboard to have students create and solve word problems. Show students a supply of two different sizes of cookie cutouts. Then ask students to brainstorm several imaginative word problems involving the mouse, little cookies, and big cookies. Note each problem on the chalkboard. Have students manipulate the cookie cutouts to arrive at the answer for each problem. Write (or have students write) the answers on the board.

Beth Persinger—Gr. K/1 • Marvin Pittiman Lab School
Statesboro, GA

Anno's Counting Book
Anno's Counting Book Big Book

Written & Illustrated by Mitsumasa Anno
Published by HarperCollins Children's Books

The kindergarten teacher who sent us this suggestion, Joanne Schlegel, says that if you could only have one book to use in teaching math concepts, the one to use is Anno's Counting Book. *It's available as a big book, too.*

Hidden within the guise of this simple picture book are lots of opportunities for math-related discussions. Choose to use the book to start discussions about one-to-one correspondence, patterns, shapes, time, measurement, and problem solving. Take your pick and dive in! If you don't have a copy of the big book, but want to share the illustrations with a group of students, use an opaque projector to project them onto a screen.

Joanne Schlegel—Gr. K • Manito School • Oakland, NJ

Millions Of Cats
Written and Illustrated by Wanda Gág
Published by Putnam Publishing Group

In this 1928 classic, a little old man sets out to find a sweet little fluffy cat for a pet. But his eyes are bigger than his pet care potential. Much to his wife's dismay, he brings home hundreds, thousands, millions, billions, and trillions of cats! It's a "cat-astrophe"!

Cats in numbers such as these are crying out to be counted! Provide a cat cutout for each student. Have students discuss the appearances of cats, before having each child color his cat cutout just like the prettiest cat he's ever seen. On a chalkboard grid, have students post their cats by color(s). What cat color(s) are favored by your class, according to the graph?

one　two　three　four　five

Make Way For Ducklings
Written and Illustrated by Robert McCloskey
Published by Puffin Books

In this Caldecott Medal classic, a pair of wild mallards arrive in busy Boston to find a home and start a family. Trying to survive amid scurrying people and hurrying machines proves to be a challenge.

Ducklings coming through! Give each student several duck-shaped crackers, glue, and construction paper. Have him glue his ducks in a row. Then, depending on your youngsters' practice needs, have them number the ducks, or copy the corresponding number or ordinal words beneath the ducks.

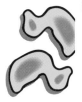

Ten Little Rabbits

Written by Virginia Grossman & Illustrated by Sylvia Long
Published by Chronicle Books

Ten active rabbits help your youngsters count to ten. They can also teach them a great deal about Native American crafts and skills.

As you read the story, discuss what the busy bunnies are doing on each page. Make a list of at least five action words (*riding, dancing, looking,* etc.) from the book. Then have students work together to propose an action word that rhymes with each of the original action words. For example, some rhyming pairs might be *walk* and *talk, cook* and *look,* and *hop* and *drop.* Once these pairs have been listed, write the following two poetry lines on the board: One little rabbit likes to _____. Two little rabbits like to _____. Then have students supply a rhyming word pair for the blanks. Continue having students create eight more lines of poetry by repeating the first two lines modified with sequential number words and additional rhyming-word pairs. When the tenth line is finished, have students read their original poem along with you.

Ten Little Rabbits proves it can be lots of fun to count with rabbits. Extend this thought by having each youngster contribute to a bunny number line. Duplicate the blanket-covered bunny on page 60. After referring to the handmade blankets in the book, have each youngster color his blanket and rabbit. Encourage each youngster to use miscellaneous craft supplies to create the bunny face. For the number line, you'll also need numerals from one through the number equal to your enrollment. Assign each student a numeral and provide him with the necessary tracer(s) so that he can trace and cut out the numeral. Display the rabbits in a row and attach the numerals in sequence below the rabbits. Once this number line is in place, your youngsters will have a ready reference for counting or adding.

One little rabbit likes to _____.
Two little rabbits like to _____.
Three little rabbits like to _____.
Four little rabbits like to _____.
Five little rabbits like to _____.

Rabbit Pattern

Use with *Ten Little Rabbits* on page 59.

Eating Fractions

Cooked, Written, Drafted, & Photo-Illustrated by Bruce McMillan
Published by Scholastic Inc.

Fractions are transformed into delectable fun with this simple, photo-illustrated treat. But be forewarned. Looking at these mouthwatering fraction recipes probably won't be good enough for your little chefs. They'll want to cook and sample them, too!

As your youngsters look at each photo in *Eating Fractions,* have them discuss what the children might be saying. Help your students brainstorm brief dialogue for each picure of a child, focusing on what the comments might be regarding the food. Write the dialogue on a Post-it® Brand note and place it on the page near the child associated with the comment. Then read the dialogue from the beginning to the end of the book. Your students' comments will undoubtedly bring new dimensions to the book.

Use the foods in the story to inspire some fabulous food fun. Either help your students make Bruce's Pepper Pizza Pie (recipe at the back of the book) or make mini pizzas on English muffin halves. Have students cut the pizzas into fourths as shown in the story. For a second course, offer banana halves. Use the recipe in the back of the book to make Bruce's Cloverleaf Rabbit Rolls and serve them divided into thirds to complete your classroom snack.

Count-a-Saurus

Written by Nancy Blumenthal
Illustrated by Robert Jay Kaufman
(This book is out of print. Check your library.)

Dinosaur enthusiasts will really get a kick out of this clever counting book. Each number is represented by a different type of prehistoric creature, and each creature is factually described in an "append-a-saurus" at the end of the book.

After reading aloud *Count-a-Saurus,* make an enormous number-line border for your classroom. Cut out a number of very large, construction-paper dinosaur shapes. Number the cutouts; then sequence them in a line around your room. When working with numeration, your dinosaur number line will certainly draw a lot of interest.

Inspired by the rhyme and rhythm of the text of *Count-a-Saurus,* your youngsters will be primed to make up their own version of this counting rhyme. Brainstorm several different dinosaur subjects for the rhyme and focus on a topic or location such as playing on a playground. As students invent each line of verse, write it on chart paper. When the verse is done, provide colorful plastic dinosaur counters or dyed dinosaur-shaped pasta. Have students manipulate the counters or pasta, creating a set to represent each numeral mentioned in their rhyme.

Chicka Chicka Boom Boom
Written by Bill Martin, Jr., & John Archambault
Illustrated by Lois Ehlert
Published by Simon & Schuster Children's Books

Use this individual activity as a follow-up to a reading of *Chicka Chicka Boom Boom* by Bill Martin, Jr. and John Archambault. It's fun for each youngster to make and provides opportunities to practice numeral seriation, numeral formation, and creative storytelling. To make one Numeral Tree, cut or tear a long construction-paper trunk and several construction-paper leaves and coconuts. Glue the trunk, leaves, and coconuts (vertically) to a large sheet of construction paper. Duplicate the numeral card patterns (page 64) onto construction paper. Trace each of the numerals with fluorescent Elmer's® GluColors™. When the glue is dry, cut the numeral cards apart.

To do this activity, a youngster traces each of the numerals (with his finger) along the raised glue line. Next he "climbs" the numerals in order up the coconut tree. Encourage each youngster to think of an original story involving the numerals and the coconut tree. Ask youngsters to create new ways that the numbers might climb up the tree such as backwards from ten or two-by-two.

Ten Bears In My Bed: A Goodnight Countdown
Written & Illustrated by Stan Mack
Published by Pantheon Books

Teddy Grahams® provide the manipulative magic for this activity. For each youngster, fold and staple a sheet of construction paper to form a pocket as shown. Have each youngster decorate his pocket to resemble a bed, then place ten Teddy Grahams® atop the "bed." Have youngsters join you in counting the number of bears; then, as you read the story aloud, have them manipulate their bears as indicated in the story. Each time another bear leaves the bed, pause to count the remaining bears. When the story is over, have each youngster tuck his bears in their bed before snacking on additional crackers and juice. As a follow-up, have youngsters take their teddy-filled beds home and tell the story to their families.

Lenora Meyer—Gr. K, Ezra Millard School, Omaha, NE

Patterns

Use with *Chicka Chicka Boom Boom* on page 63.

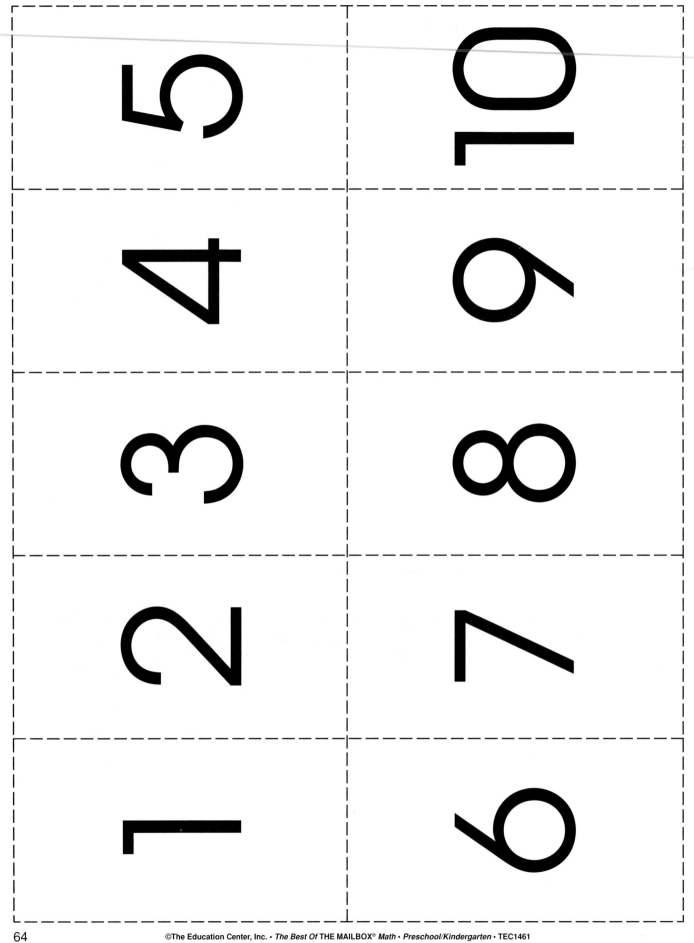

The Grouchy Ladybug
Written & Illustrated by Eric Carle
Published by HarperCollins Children's Books

From sunrise to sunset, this little spotted insect challenges everyone and anyone to fight. After a full day of badgering and bullying, the grouchy ladybug finally meets its match in the most unlikely of formidable opponents. *The Grouchy Ladybug* is a valuable classroom book in that it is an ideal literature connection to subjects such as time, insects, and manners. In addition to all that, youngsters are captivated and amused by the story and illustrations.

After sharing aloud *The Grouchy Ladybug,* have your class make this accordion-style big book to reinforce sequencing events and time concepts. Cut 18 large sheets of identically sized poster board. Program each of 17 of the sheets with a clock face showing a different time from the story. Adding the remaining page to the front for a cover, tape all of the pages in chronological order. (Tape them side-by-side so that they will fold accordion-style.) For each of the pages, assign a child (or small group of children) to examine the clock face on the big book page and match it to a clock face from *The Grouchy Ladybug.* Then have him illustrate that particular story event on a separate sheet of art paper. (Also ask one child/group to create illustrations for the title page.) When each child's illustration is complete, have him cut out and glue his illustrations to the appropriate page of the big book. During a group reading time, have young-sters share their pages and retell the story in their own words.

Gerry Porter—Gr. K, St. Aloysius, East Liverpool, OH

Rooster's Off To See The World
Written & Illustrated by Eric Carle
Published by Picture Book Studio

This selection from the Carle collection is a real winner for children who are ready to begin thinking mathematically. With brilliantly inviting collage illustra-tions, Eric Carle takes the young reader on a trip with Rooster—who has decided one morning that he'd like to travel! As he travels, Rooster is joined by animal com-panions who come in sets of two, three, four, and five. Over the course of the story, he is subsequently aban-doned by these companions—once again in sets, but this time in descending order.

Prepare this center activity to be used in conjunction with *Rooster's Off To See The World.* You will need ten large, blank index cards. Glue one rooster cutout (or photocopy) on one of the cards, two cat cutouts on another card, three frog cutouts on a third card, and so on. Then label each of the five remaining cards with a different numeral from one to five. Place the prepared cards and a copy of the book in a center. To use this center, a child may match the numerals to the sets, sequence the cards in numerical order, or retell the story using the cards as storytelling pieces.

Tracey Gest—Gr. K, J. Houston Elementary, Austin, TX

Swimmy

Written & Illustrated by Leo Lionni
Published by Alfred A. Knopf Books For Young Readers

After reading *Swimmy,* have each child draw (or trace) and cut out a large fish shape. At random, write six numerals between one and ten on each child's cutout. To play, call out numbers at random. Have each student cover the corresponding numerals with fish-shaped crackers. The first students to cover all of their numerals win the first round. Repeat the game as long as time permits. Allow youngsters to eat their fish crackers after you've played a few times.

Richelle Kreber and Sharon Roop—Gr. K
Slate Hill Elementary School
Worthington, OH

Inch By Inch

Written & Illustrated by Leo Lionni
Published by HarperCollins Children's Books

Encourage your children to explore the concept of measurement! Share the book *Inch By Inch* by Leo Lionni. After discussing the story, give each child a construction-paper worm. (For easier handling, adjust the size of the worms to your students' abilities.) Then encourage children to freely explore your classroom, measuring as they go. Provide a supply of paper and pencils for those children wishing to record their discoveries.

As a culminating activity, have students measure each other. Give each child a long strip of bulletin-board paper (at least four inches wide to allow for drawing space). Working in pairs, have one child lie down while the other child aligns the paper strip along the length of the first child. Assist each child in cutting the paper strip to match the length of his partner. Have each child write his name and draw a self-portrait at the top of his paper strip. Then mount all of the strips along a classroom wall.

Terry Schreiber and Grace Betz—Gr. K
Holy Family School
Norwood, NJ

Shayna

Toby

Read aloud *Inch By Inch.* Then give each youngster a laminated worm cutout. Encourage youngsters to measure classroom furniture and toys to determine how many worms long each item is. Then take youngsters outside and have them find out how many worms long the playground equipment is. To extend this type of activity into youngsters' homes, send notes of explanation home with the worms. It's a lively way to integrate langauage arts and the mathematical skill of measuring with nonstandard units.

Karen Galvin—Preschool, St. Clair Co-op Nursery
St. Clair, MI

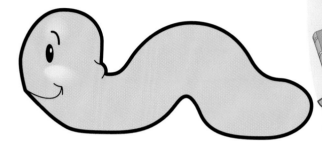

After reading *Inch By Inch* to your youngsters, have students use specially prepared inchworms to measure classroom objects. To make a worm, cut thick green craft yarn into one-inch lengths. Glue on two tiny wiggle eyes (or pom-poms) and dip the yarn ends in glue, if desired, to prevent fraying. When the glue has dried, present one of these inchworms to each student and encourage him to measure books, shoes, scissors, and other classroom objects with the help of his worm. Then have each youngster express in complete sentences his observations about the lengths of the things that he measured. For example, "My pencil is about five inches long." What a fun-filled way to introduce standard measurement!

Cathy Conery—Gr. K, Martin Park School, Boulder, CO

Jump, Frog, Jump!

Written by Robert Kalan
Illustrated by Byron Barton
Published by Greenwillow Books

Your little ones will leap into this fun-filled activity after you share *Jump, Frog, Jump!* Program each of 20 lily-pad cutouts with a different numeral from 1 to 20 and each of 20 frog cutouts with a different number word from 1 to 20. Place the lily pads in a circle on the floor and the frogs on a nearby table. Play lively music as your youngsters walk around the lily pads. Then stop the music and have each student pick up the lily pad closest to him, identify the numeral, and jump that many times. Next have each child find the frog cutout with the number word that matches his numeral. After replacing the frogs and lily pads, begin the music again and continue playing in the same manner.

Debbie Korytoski—Gr. K, Pine Ridge Elementary
Ellerslie, GA

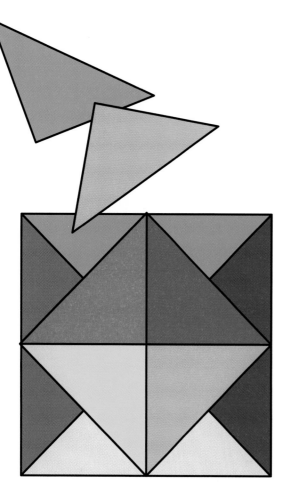

The Quilt Story

Written by Tony Johnston
Illustrated by Tomie dePaola
Published by Putnam Publishing Group

Choosing quilts as a theme is a splendid way to cover many areas of the curriculum. One great way to start is to read aloud *The Quilt Story.* Following a discussion of quilts and their designs, encourage children to bring quilts from home (with parental permission). While students' quilts are on display in your classroom, provide patterning blocks and ask students to make quiltlike designs using the blocks. Later provide paper cut to resemble the shapes of patterning blocks, and instruct students to glue the pieces onto a paper square to resemble a quilted pattern. Then glue each of the students' squares onto bulletin-board paper to make a large paper quilt for display.

Ann Stowell and Bonnie Stickler—Gr. K
Lake Elementary
Gunnison, Co

The Mitten

Written by Alvin R. Tresselt & Illustrated by Yaroslava Mills
Published by Morrow Junior Books

After reading *The Mitten,* your youngsters will get a kick out of doing this activity that reinforces counting and fine-motor skills at the same time. Photocopy the mitten cards (page 70) onto construction paper. Program each mitten with a different numeral from 1 to 9. Then laminate and cut apart the cards. Place the cards in a learning center along with 45 small blocks. To do this activity, a child places the cards on a flat surface. First he reads the numeral on a mitten; then he stacks that many blocks on top of that mitten. He continues in the same manner until all of the blocks are stacked on the mittens. And then—of course—"Aaaaa-aaaaa-aaaaa-ca-chew!" He knocks them all down!

This sequencing center can go as high as your little ones can count! Photocopy several copies of the mitten cards (page 70) onto construction paper. Program each mitten with a numeral; then laminate and cut apart the cards. Store the cards in a decorated string-tie envelope. To use this center, a child sequences the cards in numerical order.

You can have many mitten manipulatives in no time at all! Photocopy a large supply of the mitten cards (Page 70) onto colorful construction paper. Laminate the cards; then cut them apart. Place all of the cards in a center, and have each child use the mitten manipulatives as counters for working simple addition and/or subtraction problems.

Mitten Cards

Use with *The Mitten* on page 69.

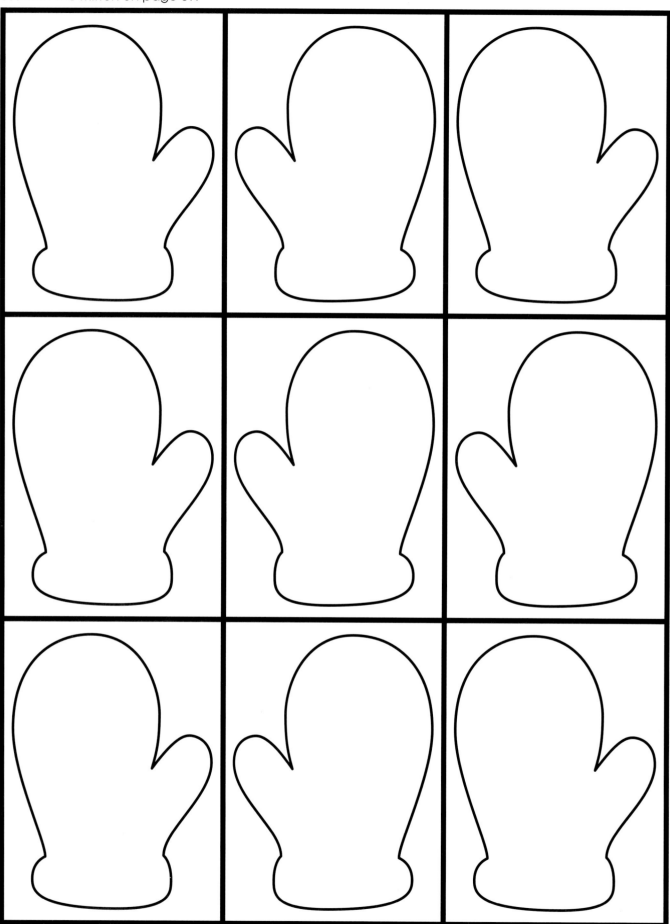

Math Games & Group Activities

Hangin' Around

Prepare this game in advance and you'll have a perfect activity for a rainy day or when you're just hangin' around for a minute or two. Program laminated seasonal cutouts with numerals. Hang each of the cutouts from the ceiling. Ask a child or group of children to find a given numeral by standing directly under that numeral. As youngsters' abilities develop, increase the level of difficulty in your directions. For example, you could say, "Find the sum of two plus three," or "All of the eights switch places with all of the fives."

Janette Anderson, Fremont, CA

Phone Number Bingo

The phones won't stop ringing—and that's just the way you'll want it! For each youngster, program a tagboard card with her phone number on one side and her name on the other. Prepare a set of calling cards (each labeled with a numeral from "zero" through "nine") and a supply of markers. To play, the caller chooses and announces a numeral. Each player who has that numeral in her phone number places a marker on that numeral. When a player has a marker on each numeral in her phone number, she calls out, "Ring!" Continue playing until all the "phones" have rung. For variety, flip each of the cards over and use alphabet calling cards to play Name Bingo.

Stephanie DeLoach—Gr. K, West Side Kindergarten
Magnolia, AR

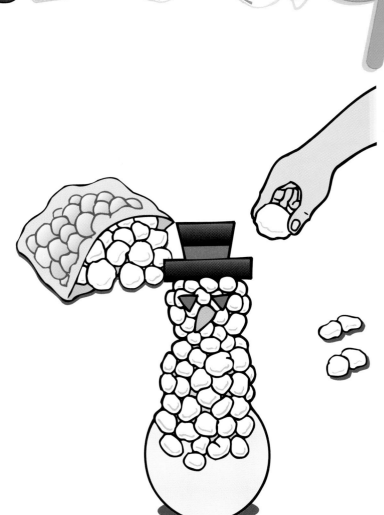

Estimation Station

Count, compare, and estimate with a little help from a "frosty" friend. From white poster board, cut a snowman shape. Display the snowman cutout and have children guess how many cotton balls it will take to fill the cutout. Starting with the "head," glue cotton balls onto the poster board while counting in unison. When the cutout is full, have children compare the actual number of cotton balls with their estimated numbers. Just for fun, glue student-made construction-paper features onto the snowman and display him over a math station in your room.

Kathleen Darby, Cumberland, RI

Mr. Buttons

With Mr. Buttons on hand, you'll always have a great math exercise to divert your youngsters to on short notice. To prepare for this transition activity, select a popular puppet to name Mr. Buttons. Display him in plain view along with a lidded container of buttons. To play, slip Mr. Buttons on your hand and have him introduce himself to your students. Then have Mr. Buttons plunge his muzzle into the container of buttons and come out with a mouthful. Give students an opportunity to guess the number of buttons in Mr. Buttons's mouth. Then have youngsters work together to count the buttons to see how close they came to the actual number. Allow students to take turns manipulating Mr. Buttons during this activity.

Michele Bolza—Gr. K
Francis H. Sheckler Elementary School
Catasauqua, PA

"My Big Glass Jar": A Number Song

Numeral recognition and counting skills come into play in this little jingle. Program each of five large cards with a different numeral from one to five. Provide a large, transparent glass jar and a supply of objects to use as counters. Sing the first verse of the song. As you begin the second verse, place the appropriate numeral card in the jar. Choose a child to place the respective amount of counters in the jar. When the song is over, remove the counter and the card; then repeat the process for each number.

(sung to the tune of "The Muffin Man")

Look and see my big glass jar,
My big glass jar, my big glass jar.
Look and see my big glass jar
As empty as can be.

Now I have the number one,
The number one, the number one.
Now I have the number one
In my big glass jar.

Paula Laughtland, Edmonds, WA

How Many Dots?

Use brightly colored stick-on dots to help you teach beginning measurement concepts. Attach a straight row of dots to a chalkboard, wall, or other flat surface. Using the row of dots as a nonstandard form of measurement, have youngsters randomly choose classroom items such as their pencils, pieces of chalk, blocks, and erasers to measure against the row of dots. Have each child verbalize or record how many dots long each of his objects is. If you have an abundance of dot stickers, consider making a vertical row of dots long enough for children to use to measure each other. Gee, how many dots are you?

Shelia Brown—Gr. K
Ford Elementary
St. Louis, MO

Musical Shapes

Step in time in a line. Listen to the beat; then take a seat! In advance, laminate two sets of a classroom quantity of construction-paper shapes. Keep one of the sets for yourself, and from the other set, give one shape to each child. Arrange children's chairs in musical-chairs fashion. To play, have children march in a wide circle around the chairs as music plays. While the children march, place a shape from your set of shapes on each of the chairs. Whenever you like, stop the music and each child scatters to be seated in a chair displaying a shape that matches his shape. As children's abilities permit, redistribute the shapes and play again.

Mary Jo Morrissey—Pre-K, Preschool Playhouse—YMCA
Little Falls, NY

Roll For Beans

Rolling for beans reinforces many skills including matching colors, sorting, counting, one-to-one correspondence, and graphing. Each player needs a tagboard strip on which ten bean shapes have been drawn in a row. This is the "bank" where he places his beans. Provide spray-painted, dried beans in six bright, acrylic colors and a die or cube with matching colors.

To play, one child rolls the die and selects a bean of the color shown on the top of the die. He places his bean on one of the bean shapes on his tagboard strip. The next child rolls the die and does the same. Play continues until each player has filled his or her "bank." The players can then graph their beans on large graphing paper.

To reinforce the ideas of "counting on" and simple addition, use two regular dice and change the total number of beans in the bank.

Rita Thorson—Gr. K
St. Patrick's School
Cedar Rapids, IA

75

The Numbers Game

Looking for a math exercise to fill a few minutes? Here's one that little ones will enjoy. Have students stand in a circle. Then have youngsters count off, stopping at a specified number. The child who calls out the specified number sits down. For example, if the specified number is four, youngsters count, "One, two, three, four," and the youngster who said "four" sits down. The count begins at one again, and play continues in this manner until each youngster is seated. When youngsters are more proficient with their numeration skills, ask them to count by tens, fives, or twos.

Bobbie Hallman—Gr. K
Burbank School
Merced, CA

Dot-To-Dot Activity

Youngsters will learn numeral recognition and sequencing on the spot with this active version of dot-to-dot. For each numeral that you wish to include in this game, make a numeral card that is large enough to be seen at a distance (across your room, for example). Give each of the cards to a different child; then have the card-holding children scatter to random areas of your classroom. Choose a youngster to act as the pencil and walk in numerical order from child to child based on the numeral card that each child is holding.

For extra fun, give the pencil person a ball of yarn. As she walks from child to child in numerical order, have her unravel the yarn, allowing each card-holding child to hold a section of the yarn as she passes. You'll soon see those sequencing skills combine with creativity as youngsters begin to position themselves in order to make clever designs!

Sherri Gustine—Gr. K, Limestone Elementary School
Grant Park, IL

"Stringing" Popcorn

This fast-paced game produces a "string" of number-sequencing practice. Thread a popcorn cutout onto a yarn necklace for each child. Beginning with the number *one,* program each cutout with a different number. (Depending on your youngsters' counting skills, you may wish to separate them into smaller groups and make several identical sets using only the numbers *one* to *five* or *one* to *ten*.) Slip a necklace around each youngster's neck. To "string" popcorn, have students randomly hop around the room, imitating kernels of corn popping. When you call, "Make a string!", have youngsters hop to arrange themselves in numerical order, then join hands. Pop! Pop! Pop!

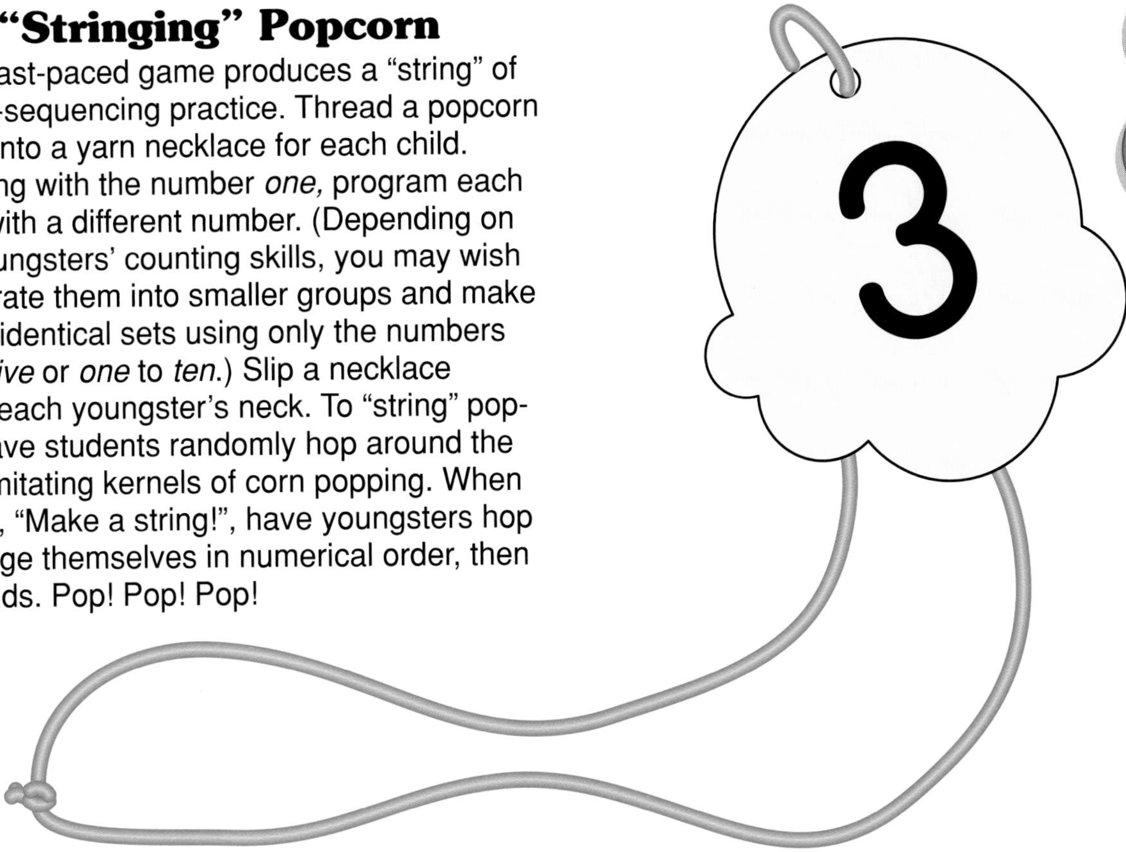

Magic Number

Improvise with this math game when you've got a few minutes between activities. Write a number on a scrap of paper. Fold the paper and attach it to your blackboard with a magnet. Beneath the magnet draw and number a number line. Ask your youngsters to guess the magic number that you have written on the paper. When a number is guessed, mark it on the number line; then tell youngsters whether the magic number is higher or lower than (greater than or less than) the number guessed. Continue marking students' guesses on the number line until the magic number is called. Unfold the paper to confirm that the number is correct. Children enjoy trying to guess the number with as few guesses as possible.

Mona Nale—Gr. K
Evergreen Elementary
Midlothian, VA

Number Line Hop

Hopping along a giant floor number line is a great way to practice gross-motor skills while beefing up math skills. To prepare for this activity, attach masking tape to the classroom floor so that it extends in a straight line for several feet. Number each of several index cards and attach them sequentially at even intervals along the tape. For durability, adhere each card to the floor using a rectangle of clear Con-Tact® covering that is a bit larger than the card. When the number line is finished, have students take turns hopping, skipping, and galloping along it. Or play a number song and have a student hop to each numeral as it is mentioned in the song.

Sheila Leath
Allendale Primary School
Allendale, SC

Seven Up

A roll of the die adds up to fun! In advance, explain to youngsters that the numbers on the opposite sides of a die add up to seven. Then have a youngster roll a die and call out the number he rolls. Challenge him to use his mathematical reasoning skills to determine the number on the other side of the die, then lift the die to verify his answer. Seven up!

Connie Lennert—Gr. K, Kingsley School
Downers Grove, IL

Roll And Count

This transition activity is great counting practice and exercise. In advance, locate a pair of large foam-rubber dice. The when time permits, select a child to toss the dice. He may count the total number of dots or add the numbers represented by both dice. When the sum of the dice has been identified, have the child choose an exercise or movement that can be done that number of times. If the sum of the dice was six, for example, he could do six jumping jacks along with this classmates.

Sherry Griffin—Gr. K
Hester School
Farmersville, CA

Sweet Math Manipulatives

Use these seasonal gameboards to reinforce addition and subtraction skills. To make an "eggboard," glue three pastel-colored egg shapes on the front and on the back of a piece of construction paper. Be sure to leave space between the eggs to program with plus, minus, and equal signs. Laminate the board. To use this activity, supply each child with an eggboard, a quantity of jelly beans, a tissue, and a wipe-off crayon. Direct each child to turn his board to the side with the plus sign. Have him put a designated set of jelly beans in the first egg and a set in the second egg. Have him add the two sets of jelly beans, then write his answer in the third egg using a wipe-off crayon. Check each board for accuracy. Have each student use the tissue to wipe off the answer. Continue in the same manner using different numbers each time; then have students use the backs of the boards for subtraction problems. Allow your youngsters to munch on some jelly beans after the activity is completed.

Sherri L. Gustine—Gr. K
Limestone Elementary
Kankakee, IL

Up, Up, And Take-Away

Watch the excitement in your classroom soar when reinforcing subtraction skills with this approach. Attach an extra long length of curling ribbon to each of five helium balloons. (Make the ribbons long enough so that your students can easily pull the balloons down from the ceiling.) Select one youngster to stand in the front of the room holding all five of the balloons. Have a student volunteer tell the youngster how many balloons to release. After the released balloons float to the ceiling, guide your class in verbalizing a correlating subtraction story such as: "Connie had five balloons, but two floated away. How many does she have left?" Repeat this process until all of the children have had a chance to hold and release the balloons.

Cheryl A. Wade—Gr. K

Addition And Subtraction Storytelling

Make word problems a sweet treat by using M&M's®. Have students add and subtract sets with M&M's®; then make up a word problem to go with each one. As a follow-up activity, encourage your students to write number sentences to go with their word problems.

Kathleen Schwab—Gr. K
Brooklyn Elementary
Brooklyn, CT

Graphing Activity

After sharing a birthday-related literature selection, have each child use crayons and markers to decorate a personalized birthday-cake cutout. Write a different month of the year on each of 12 sentence strips. Position the sentence strips on your floor to serve as labels for a floor graph. When each child hears her birth month spoken as you chorally recite the birthday rhyme (see the illustration), have her graph her cutout above the appropriate month. When the graph is complete, discuss what it reveals.

Vicki Altland—Gr. K, Florence Mattison Elementary, Conway, AR

Hannah

Apples, peaches, pears, and plums; Tell me when your birthday comes. (Say the months of the year.)

Shark Bites® Graph

This nifty hands-on graphing activity sure has lots of bite! Create a graph with a column for each of the colors found in Shark Bites® fruit snacks. Give each child a copy of the graph and a small Ziploc® sandwich bag containing some Shark Bites®. Have each youngster graph his assortment of Shark Bites®. Then have each youngster interpret and explain his graph. Allow your students to eat the sharks after this fun-filled activity.

Cheryl A. Wade—Gr. K
Golden Springs Elementary
Oxford, AL

Sh-Sh-Sh-Shark!

red	orange	purple	green	yellow	white

Money-Recognition Idea

This money-recognition idea is sure to make "cents" in your classroom. Enlarge pictures of a penny, nickel, dime, and quarter to make giant-size coins. Cut out the face of the president on each coin. Pick student volunteers to peer through openings in the penny, nickel, dime, and quarter as you read these poems aloud:

Poem for the penny:
See the shiny penny, brown as it can be,
Showing Abe Lincoln for all of us to see.
He had a bushy beard and a tall black hat.
A penny's worth one cent. How about that?

Poem for the dime:
A dime is the smallest coin of them all,
With Roosevelt posing nice and tall.
A dime is worth ten cents. Don't you agree?
Which makes Roosevelt as happy as can be!

Karen Cook—Gr. K
McDonough Primary School
McDonough, GA

Poem for the nickel:
Thomas Jefferson will be found
On a nickel, shiny, smooth, and round.
His home, Monticello, is on the other side.
A nickel is worth five cents. Say it with pride.

Poem for the quarter:
On the quarter, I'm sure that you will find
A man who was a leader, honest and kind.
George Washington was our first president.
And a quarter is worth 25 cents.

The Giving Trees

Money actually *does* grow on these special holiday trees! Cut four large Christmas tree shapes from green construction paper; then mount them on a bulletin board. Top each tree with a yellow construction-paper star. Label each star with a different amount: 1¢, 5¢, 10¢, 25¢. Each day children may bring change for the money trees. Have students sort and tally each set of coins; then tape the coins to the appropriate tree. Plan for a Salvation Army representative to visit your classroom a day or two before your Christmas vacation. Children will delight in giving the money to your special visitor.

Lisa Kuecker—Gr. K
Adams Elementary
Arkansas City, KS

5¢

Lotto Fun

Use this version of the ever-popular lotto game at a small-group center and as a take-home game. Duplicate and cut out the gameboards, caller card patterns, and parent letter on pages 84 and 85. Place the gameboards and stacked caller cards at a center with a bowl of markers (such as beans, pennies, or squares of paper). To play, each child chooses a gameboard and eight markers. In turn, a child draws the top caller card and announces the numeral to be covered with a marker. When a child has covered all of the numerals on his gameboard, he calls out, "Lotto!"

To send the game home, store a set of caller cards and gameboards, a supply of markers, and the parent note in a zippered plastic bag.

Susan Osborn—Gr. K
Carrie Martin Elementary
Loveland, CO

☆☆ **Lotto Fun** ☆☆

9	2	4	10
3	6	7	5

© The Education Center, Inc. • The Best Of THE MAILBOX® Math • Preschool/Kindergarten • TEC1461

The Twelve Days Of Christmas

This tree-trimming game can be adapted in a variety of ways to meet the needs and abilities of your students. To play the game, you will need a book version of *The Twelve Days Of Christmas.* For each child, you will also need 12 markers—such as wrapped candies or colorful milk-jug lids—and a copy of one of the Christmas-tree playing cards (page 86). If you'd like students to play with different cards on which the numerals are randomly placed, photocopy the unprogrammed card for each child. (Always keep the original card blank so you'll be able to adapt this game as desired.) Randomly program each of the circles on the cards with a different numeral from 1–12. As you read the story, have each child place a marker on each numeral as it is mentioned in the story. After the last marker has been placed on the "12," have each child remove his markers respectively as you read, "12 lords a-leaping, 11 ladies dancing," etc.

To add a little holiday excitement (and comedy) to this game, use the randomly programmed playing cards and sing the story. As you sing together, encourage each child to notice when he has covered a three-in-a-row sequence (vertically, horizontally, or diagonally). Each time a child has three in a row, have him call out, "Happy holidays!" In response, have the class chorally say, "Happy holidays to you, too!"

adapted from an idea by Kaye Sowell—Gr. K
Pelahatchie Elementary School
Pelahatchie, MS

Lotto Fun

2	6	3	10
8	1	7	4

Lotto Fun

4	8	10	2
5	9	7	3

Lotto Fun

9	2	4	10
3	6	7	5

Lotto Fun

1	5	9	4
3	7	2	6

Patterns Use with "Lotto Fun" on page 83.

Caller cards

1	2	3	4	5
6	7	8	9	10
1	2	3	4	5
6	7	8	9	10

Parent Letter Use with "Lotto Fun" on page 83.

Dear Parent,

We have been learning to recognize numerals from one to ten. You and your child can practice recognizing numerals at home with this numeral lotto game. To play, take all of the pieces out of the bag. Have your child give each player a gameboard and eight markers. Shuffle the caller cards; then choose one person to be the caller. Stack the caller cards facedown. The caller turns over the top caller cards and announces the numeral. Any player who has that numeral on his gameboard marks that space with a marker. Continue playing in this manner. When a player has a marker on each of the spaces on his gameboard, he calls out, "Lotto!"

Have fun learning and playing!

Math Learning Centers

A Box Of Chocolates

Use a heart-shaped box of chocolates for a sweet review of shapes. Remove the chocolates from the candy divider. Using markers or shape stickers, label each section of the divider or each even interval of the box bottom with a shape(s). In the same manner, program the bottoms of chocolate kisses with shapes to match those in the candy box. Place the chocolates in a resealable plastic bag. Place the bag and the empty candy box in a center with a bowl of chocolate kisses. To use this center, a child takes each piece of chocolate from the bag and places it on the corresponding page in the box. After all of the chocolates have been placed, allow the youngster to enjoy a chocolate kiss from the bowl.

adapted from an idea by Dawn Spurck—Director
Creative Play Center
Colorado Springs, CO

Turkey Shape Match

Here's a gobblin' good shape-matching activity that keeps in stride with the turkey mood. On a large sheet of poster board, draw shapes that have quite a bit of space between them (see the illustration). For each shape, make an identical shape cutout. To each of the shapes on the poster board, add a turkey head and wattle, feathers, and feet. Attach one side of a small piece of Velcro® to each of the poster-board turkeys and the other side of the Velcro® to each of the shape cutouts. To do this activity, a youngster matches each shape cutout to the turkey with the same-shape body, then sticks the two sides of Velcro® together.

Beth Taylor Devlin—Pre-K Special Education
Dutch Lane Elementary School
Hicksville, NY

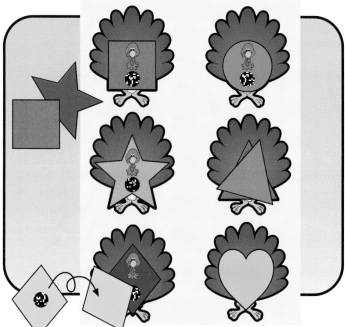

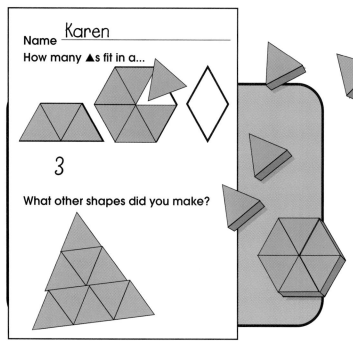

Transforming Triangles

Your youngsters' problem-solving skills will be in tip-top shape after working out at this pattern-block center. In advance, cut a large quantity of green paper triangles that are identical in size to pattern-block triangles. Then trace the trapezoid, hexagon, and diamond pattern blocks onto a sheet of paper. (If desired, add to the page as shown.) Duplicate the page on construction paper for each child; then place the prepared pages, paper triangles, glue, and a set of triangle pattern blocks in a center. Encourage each child to experiment with the triangle blocks to try to make other shapes. Then have him record his discoveries by gluing the paper triangles onto the prepared page (or a blank page) to resemble the shapes he has created. How many triangles are in a trapezoid? A hexagon? A diamond?

Wilma Droegemueller—Gr. K
Zion Lutheran School
Mt. Pulaski, IL

Math Munchies

Munch and crunch your way through this fun-filled math activity. Stock your math center with four or five plastic bags, each filled with a different kind of cereal. Also provide laminated construction-paper strips. To use this center, a child takes several pieces of cereal from each bag; then he creates a pattern with the pieces on the construction-paper strip. To vary this activity, have him sort the cereal by color, shape, or size. When a child completes this center, allow him to munch on his cereal.

Kathy Grazko—Gr. K
St. Ann School
Cleveland Heights, OH

Pattern Tubes

These pattern tubes are just the right size for manipulating. Cut paper-towel tubes into a supply of three different lengths. Spray paint the longest lengths one color, the middle lengths another color, and the shortest lengths yet another color. Make pattern cards by drawing patterns that match the colors of the tubes. When the paint is dry, place the tubes and the pattern cards in a basket in a center. Have children duplicate the patterns that are on the cards and/or create their own patterns for a center partner to duplicate.

Dr. Sandra C. Richardson—Assistant Professor
Clinch Valley College
Wise, VA

Patterning Paw Prints

Youngsters make tracks in patterning practice at this fun center. In advance, make paw-print stamps by carving a raised paw shape from a potato half. Or cut out and glue sponge pieces to a square of cardboard to resemble a paw print; then attach an empty spool to the cardboard for a handle. Place the paw-print stamps, construction paper, and several containers of different colors of paint in a center. Have students use the stamps and paints to create a variety of patterns.

Sheli Gossett
Avon Elementary
Avon Park, FL

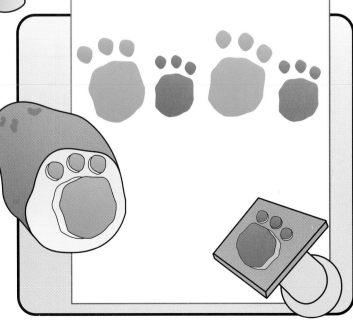

Stick To The Pattern

Using various kinds of stickers, create rows of different patterns on the inside of a file folder. In each of the patterns, leave one or some of the spaces blank by drawing square outlines in place of the stickers. Cut a supply of tagboard cards sized to fit in the squares. For each of the blanks in a pattern, make an answer card by sticking the correct sticker on one side of a card and an incorrect sticker on the other side. For each pattern, have a child find the correct answer card(s) and place it (them) in the appropriate place(s) in the pattern. As youngsters' skills progress, develop more complicated patterns.

Linda Chapman—Gr. K
Summertown Elementary
Summertown, TN

Pasta Patterning

Pasta adds pizzazz to patterning! Squeeze 10–15 drops of food coloring into each of several bottles of rubbing alcohol. Pour each bottle of alcohol into a different large bowl. Soak rigatoni in each bowl of colored alcohol overnight until the desired color is achieved. Remove the pasta and place it on paper towels to dry. When the pasta is dry, place each color in a separate bowl. Using matching colored sticky dots, program poster-board cards with different patterns. Laminate the cards for durability. To create stringers, dip the ends of yarn lengths in glue; then allow them to harden. Place the cards, bowls of pasta, and stringers in a center.

A youngster selects a card and strings pasta to match. He then continues the same pattern until his stringer is filled. If desired, assist each youngster in tying the loose ends of his stringer together to create a necklace or belt.

Nancy Farlow
St. Joseph, MO

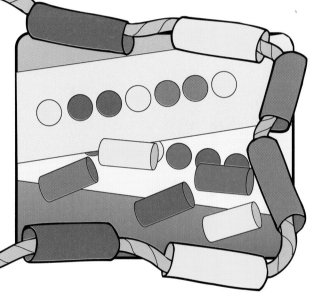

Pretty Patterns

Easter eggs lend a manipulative seasonal flair to this patterning center. Provide a basket of assorted colors of plastic eggs and a few empty egg cartons. Cut construction-paper egg shapes in colors that match your plastic eggs. Glue the egg shapes in various patterns onto tagboard cards. Have a youngster select a pattern card, then extend the pattern by placing the plastic eggs in an egg carton. A youngster may also create an original pattern for a classmate to repeat or identify.

Kaye Sowell—Gr. K
Pelahatchie Elementary School
Pelahatchie, MS

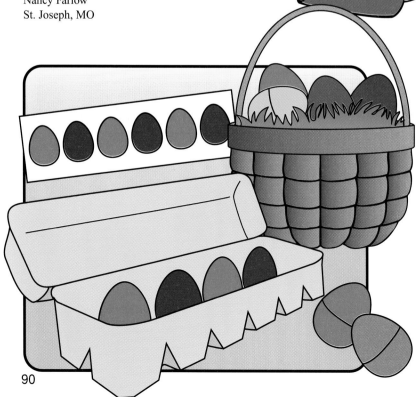

Clip-Ons

Young children will enjoy making their hands look like the illustrations on these number cards, and they will also strengthen their fine-motor muscles as they practice a little one-to-one correspondence. Collect a supply of mini clothespins. Duplicate the patterns on page 101. (If you are going to use regular-sized clothespins, enlarge the patterns before duplicating them.) Cut apart the cards. Mount each card on a piece of construction paper; then laminate. Store all of the cards and clothespins in a string-tie envelope. To use this center, a youngster chooses a card, then clips clothespins onto the card to match the number represented.

Paula Finne—Preschool Special Education
Zumbrota Elementary School
Zumbrota, MN

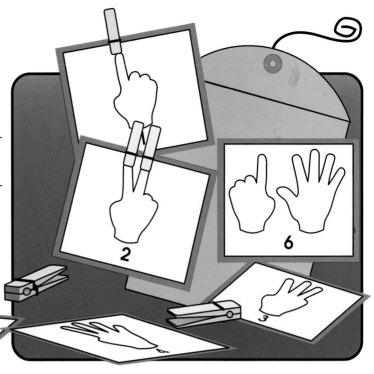

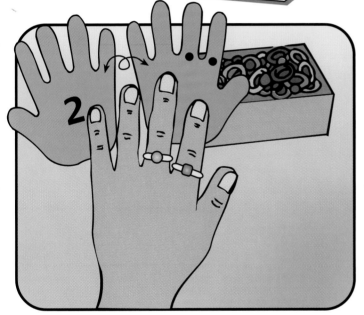

Hands-On Math

Here's a handy idea for practice with a number of math skills. Cut out a supply of hand shapes from tagboard. Write a numeral or number word on one side of the hand. On the other side of the hand, attach brightly colored dots on the fingers to resemble rings. Place the hands and a supply of toy rings in the center. When a youngster visits the center, he selects a hand cutout and looks at the numeral or number word. He then places the correct number of rings on his own hand. To check, he flips the card over and compares the number of dots to the number of rings on his hand.

adapted from an idea by Michele Hertz—Gr. K
Central Islip Early Childhood Center
Central Islip, NY

Loading Zone

This fun center helps youngsters practice their counting skills. To make the center, design and cut out six simple school-bus patterns. (Be sure that your pattern has a large window space, as shown.) Label each cutout with a different numeral from one to six. Attach the buses to poster board or a bulletin board, leaving the bottom edges of the windows open to create pockets. Provide enough smiley-face cutouts to "load" each bus with the indicated amount. Store the smiley faces in a resealable plastic bag. To complete this activity, a child slides the correct number of smiley faces into each bus window.

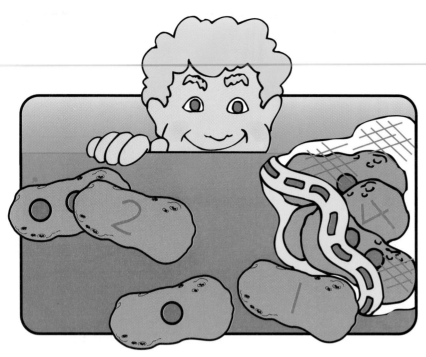

Potato Patch Matchups

Dig up a little matching fun with this versatile center. Cut out a supply of tan construction-paper potato shapes. Program each pair with matching numerals and dot sets. Code the backs for self-checking if desired; then laminate the cutouts and place them in an empty, five-pound potato bag. Matching skills will be sprouting out all over!

Liz Mooney—Gr. K
Central Rayne School
Rayne, LA

Pop, Pop, Popcorn!

Pop some fun into a math center! Provide a supply of popped popcorn and 11 large, laminated popcorn cutouts. Program each of the popcorn cutouts with a numeral from 0–10 or a number word. Have each youngster place the correct amount of popcorn pieces on each of the popcorn cutouts. How many pieces of popcorn are there altogether? Count 'em as you crunch 'em!

Maureen Cenci Busche—Gr. K
Point Park Children's School
Pittsburgh, PA

French-Fried Counting

An order of these fries adds up to counting fun. Ask a local fast-food restaurant for a donation of french-fry boxes. Program each box with a different numeral. Make "fries" by cutting yellow sponges into strips. Place the boxes and fries in a center. To do this activity, a child places the appropriate number of fries in each box.

Lesa M. Whatley—Pre/K
Family Day Care
Auburn, GA

Turkeytime Tallying

Create this counting center in a snap from disposable Thanksgiving plates. Program a set of ten disposable Thanksgiving plates with numerals from one to ten. If desired, code the backs with dot sets for self-checking. Place the plates and 55 turkey cutouts (or die-cut calendar emblems) at a center. A youngster selects a plate and places the matching number of cutouts on it. Tallyho!

Michelle Keltner—Gr. K–5
Southern Baptist Educational Center
Horn Lake, MS

Christmas Tree Counting

Here's a festive center that brings lots of holiday cheer. In advance, collect ten thread cones from textile mills. Paint the thread cones green to resemble Christmas trees. Place a dot sticker on one of the cone trees to represent an ornament. Attach two stickers to a second cone, and continue to decorate cones in this manner until the cone trees are decorated to represent sets one through ten. Program each of ten star cutouts with a different numeral from one to ten; then tape a section of a drinking straw to each star. To use this center, a child counts the dots on each tree, then places each star in the corresponding treetop. If desired, also have each chid numerically sequence the trees.

Laurie Mills—Gr. K
Stevenson Elementary
Stevenson, AL

Menorah Matchups

Light up number-recognition skills with this bright Hanukkah center. Using a marker, draw and color the base of a menorah on a sheet of poster board. Attach nine, yellow cups atop the base to represent candle holders. Program eight of the cups with the numerals one through eight, leaving the center cup unprogrammed to represent the *shammash* (lighting candle) holder. Display the menorah on a bulletin board or easel; then fill the shammash holder with 36 construction paper candles. A youngster removes the candle cutouts from the shammash holder, then places a matching number in each cup. My, what glowing counting skills!

Sheila Weinberg
Warren Point School
Fair Lawn, NJ

Old Stamps

Your youngsters' math skills are sure to improve with this "send off"! Make a slot (the width of an envelope) in the lid of a box; then decorate the box to resemble a mailbox. Cut used stamps from envelopes of old cards and letters. Glue sets of stamps onto different envelopes. On poster-board cards, write a numeral to match each of the stamp sets. Have a youngster insert a numeral card into the envelope with the corresponding set; then "mail" the envelope. Good work, Mr. Postman!

Sandra Hatton—Gr. K
Garth Elementary
Georgetown, KY

Marshmallow Smiles

This counting activity is sure to bring miles of smiles! From red construction paper, cut out ten or more mouth shapes as shown. Then mount each mouth on a different poster-board card. Program the middle of each mouth with a number or number word. Laminate the cards for durability. Place the cards and a bag of miniature marshmallows in a large, lidded can which has been decorated to resemble a stick of lip balm. A youngster spreads out the cards on a tabletop, then places the matching number of marshmallow "teeth" inside each mouth. Grin and *count* it!

Debbie Wilson—Preschool
Carmel Baptist Weekday Early Education School
Charlotte, NC

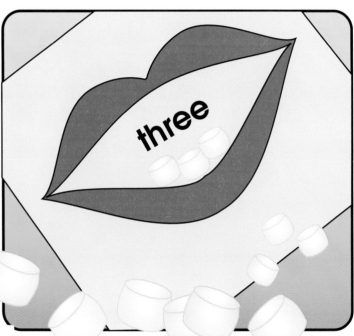

Heart-To-Heart

Youngsters will get to the heart of the matter while doing this fun math center. Cut ten large heart cutouts from white, red, or pink construction paper. Label each heart with a different numeral from one to ten. Place the cutouts and a bowl of candy conversation hearts at a center. To use this center, a child chooses a cutout, counts out the correct number of candy hearts, and places them on the cutout. Play continues in this manner until each cutout has been used. Be sure to leave extra candy hearts in another bowl for your little ones to sample!

Mylene Winchester—Director
Munchkin Manor
Easley, SC

Pots Of Gold

Your little ones will be only too eager to get their hands on this gold! Paint 11 small paper cups or nut cups black to resemble pots. Spray paint 55 (or more) beans gold. Label each of 11 shamrock cutouts with a numeral from zero to ten. Attach a labeled shamrock to each pot. To do this activity, a child puts the correct number of gold pieces in each pot. To extend the skills addressed at this center, you can have children put the shamrocks in numerical order. You can also spray paint some more beans and label a new set of shamrocks with simple addition or subtraction facts. Then attach these new shamrocks to the pots. Have children use the gold as counters and put gold pieces equivalent to the sums and differences in the appropriate pots.

Susan J. Mills
Keswick Christian School
St. Petersburg, FL

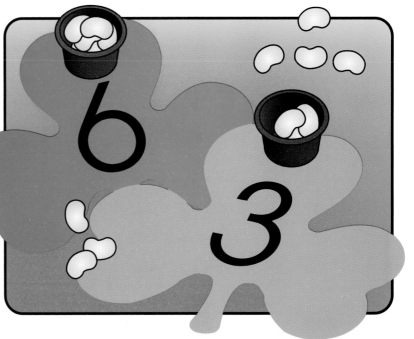

Ladybug, Ladybug

Capitalize on your little ones' fascination with ladybugs to catch their attention for some numeral and set practice. Cut ladybug shapes out of construction paper; then color and laminate them. Using a permanent marker, write a number on each of the ladybug cutouts. Paint a supply of milk jug lids black to represent ladybug spots. To use the center, have a youngster place spots on each of the ladybugs to match the indicated numeral. Adapt this center to the needs of your youngsters by programming each of the ladybugs with a number word or an addition or a subtraction fact.

Erma McGill—Pre-K
Kiowa, OK

Basketfuls Of Berries!

Try this "berry" good counting activity. In advance, collect ten strawberry baskets and program the outside of each basket with a different numeral from one to ten. Then cut out 55 strawberry shapes, or have students make them. Place the baskets and strawberries in a center. To use this center, a child first puts the baskets in numerical order, then fills each basket with the correct number of strawberries.

95

Watermelon Fun

Here's a juicy way to practice numeral recognition and counting. For each number that you would like to include in this center, make a watermelon slice by coloring the rim of half of a paper plate green, and the center section red or pink. Write a numeral on each watermelon slice. Provide a supply of dried black beans or spray paint another type of bean black. To use this center, a child chooses a slice of watermelon, reads the numeral, and then places that many seeds (beans) on the slice. As a child completes this center, have her help herself to a slice of real watermelon and count the seeds as she eats!

Jeanette Warwick—Pre-K
Berkley/Campostella Early Childhood Education Center
Norfolk, VA

Collecting Shells

Children can reinforce their counting skills while participating in a favorite summer activity—collecting shells. Program each of ten (or more) pages of a seashell notepad (or cutouts) with a different numeral. Place the programmed pages and a collection of shells in a center. To use this center, a child chooses a page, then places the indicated number of shells on or around that page. If desired, also have each child numerically sequence the pages.

Pat Johnson
United Methodist Preschool
Reynoldsburg, OH

Flag Count

Counting skills will be proudly displayed at this star-spangled center. Provide 55 (or more) party-sized flags on toothpicks. Paint ten Styrofoam® blocks with blue spray paint. Label each of ten construction-paper cards with a numeral from one to ten; then tape the cards to the Styrofoam® blocks. Have a youngster stick flags into each of the blocks to match the indicated numeral. For another challenge, have a youngster arrange each of the flag-adorned blocks in numerical order.

Vanette Hann—Gr. K
Vandalia Elementary
Greensboro, NC

Get Your Turtles In A Row

Use this manipulative activity to reinforce the concept of "one more." Duplicate five copies of the turtle patterns (page 102) on white construction paper. Color each turtle's head, legs, and tail; then color sections of the turtles' shells in increments of one. For example, the first turtle will have one colored section on his shell, the second turtle two colored sections, the third turtle three colored sections, and so on. Laminate and cut out each of the turtle patterns. To do this activity, a child sequences the turtle cutouts so that each turtle has one more colored section than the one before it.

Wilma Droegemueller—Gr. K and Preschool
Zion Lutheran School
Mt. Pulaski, IL

Bead Boards

Use these bead boards for hands-on practice with addition fact families. To make a bead board, string a desired number of beads onto a piece of yarn or string. Holding the yarn or string taut, attach each end to a piece of tagboard or cardboard. Program a supply of cards with addition facts. Group the cards into fact families; then place them in a center with one or more corresponding bead boards. Have a child choose a card, then slide the beads on the bead board according to the written math fact. If desired, provide paper and writing utensils for youngsters to write the facts and the answers they have discovered.

Susan Lind—Preschool and Gr. K
Lincoln Elementary School
Clarksville, TN

2+2=   3+1=   4+0=

Window Booklets

If you are looking for a versatile learning-center idea, take a peek at these window booklets. Cut the folded flap sections off a supply of plain and window envelopes. Program each window envelope for the skill of your choice; then program an index card with a correct match or answer for each envelope. Create a booklet to target a specific skill by stapling a plain envelope on top of several programmed envelopes. Write a title on the top envelope and store all of the answer cards for the booklet inside. Stock a center with several of these booklets. To use the center, a child selects a booklet and removes the answer cards. He then looks at a programmed envelope and inserts a matching card to peek at the answer through the window.

Pam Cook—Grs. K–1
Sumrall Elementary
Sumrall, MS

Sticker Addition

This self-checking center with a hint of the season is one more reason for learning to add! Program an addition fact (horizontally) on the bottom of each of a supply of 5" x 7" cards. On each card, above the written equation, place holiday stickers to correspond with the numerals on the card; then add the function signs. Cut the cards apart horizontally, using a different jigsaw cut on each of the cards. Have a youngster match a sticker equation to a written equation. To check his answer, the youngster simply puts the pieces together. If the pieces fit, it's a match!

Kathleen Darby—Gr. K
Cumberland, RI

Buttons, Buttons

Pop these buttons on and off for learning that really sticks! Program tagboard cards with addition facts. On the other side of each card, program a "+" and "="; then glue on small Velcro® strips to match the addends in the equation. Next, glue the complementary side of the Velcro® strips onto the backs of assorted buttons. Have a youngster stick buttons onto the Velcro® strips and count the buttons to solve each problem. To check an answer, he flips the card over.

Karen Heck—Gr. K
Holy Innocents
Chicago, IL

Bunnies In A Basket

Youngsters will enjoy hopping these little bunnies around this math center. To make a "bunny board," enlarge and duplicate the bunny pattern (page 103) onto construction paper. Color, cut out, and mount the pattern on a sheet of poster board. Duplicate the small bunny patterns (page 103) onto construction paper; then color, cut, and mount them on poster board. Make a set of cards with simple addition/subtraction problems. Provide a set of ten plastic chips to use as markers. To use the center, have a youngster choose a card and use the little bunnies as counters to determine the answer. The youngster then places a plastic chip on that numeral (the answer) on the bunny board. The youngster continues to choose problem cards until all of the numerals on the bunny board are covered.

Adapt this center into a two-person game by providing another bunny board and another set of plastic chips. In turn, have each youngster choose a problem card, then cover the appropriate numeral on his playing board. The first player to cover all of the numerals on his board is the winner.

adapted from an idea by Marie Wiseman and Patsy Lithrone—Gr. K
Appalachia Roman Catholic School
Stephenville, Newfoundland, Canada

Fruity Graph

This center provides a tasty way to pack a lot of learning into graphing fun. Draw and program a graph similar to the one shown. For each child, provide a copy of the graph, a plastic bag containing about 15 pieces of fruit-shaped cereal, and crayons. To do this activity, a child takes one bag of cereal and a graph. As she removes each piece of cereal from her bag, she colors a space in the appropriate column of her graph, then eats the cereal piece. She continues to color and crunch until all of her cereal pieces are gone. Discuss with each child what her graph reveals, and/or discuss all of the graphs during a group time.

Mary Beth Brever—Gr. K
Rawson Elementary School
South Milwaukee, WI

Roll And Graph

Use this versatile individual or partner activity to enhance a number of math skills. Create a graph with six vertical columns and seven horizontal rows (as shown). Program each space in the bottom row of the graph with a numeral (or number word or dots). Make copies of the graph to keep the center supplied. Program each of the sides of a cube with a numeral from the graph. To play, roll the die (cube); then match the numeral on the top of the die to a numeral on your graph. Color one of the spaces in that numeral's column. Roll the die several more times, graphing each result. After a few minutes of this, examine and interpret the graph.

Mary Nelson—Gr. K
Arthur Elementary
Cedar Rapids, IA

Unscrambled Eggs

Graphing skills are on the rise with this Easter Egg encounter. Fill a basket with an assortment of four colors of plastic Easter eggs. For each youngster, duplicate the graph on page 104; then place the basket of eggs and the graphs in a center. Have a youngster sort the eggs by color, then color the graph accordingly. For "egg-stra" good workers, fill a large plastic egg with a seasonal treat. Allow each youngster to take a treat from the egg when he has completed the center.

Kaye Sowell—Gr. K

99

Around The Clock

Here's a center game to reinforce clock numeral placement. For each gameboard, glue a construction-paper clock to a colored background. Label each of several chips (in sets of 12 chips) with a numeral from 1 to 12. In turn, have each player roll a 12-sided die, then cover that numeral on his clock with the correctly labeled chip. If a player rolls a numeral that has already been covered with a chip, he passes the die to the next player. Continue playing until all of the numerals on each clock are covered.

Elke DuPree—Gr. K
Shallowford Falls
Marietta, GA

Special Delivery!

Need a "heart-y" way for youngsters to write and send valentines? If so, set up a post office center in your classroom. In advance, stock your center with valentines, envelopes, construction paper, stickers (to represent stamps), coins, a cash register, and a cardboard mailbox. Attach programmed price tags to items such as the paper, valentines, stamps, and envelopes.

To use this center, have three youngsters visit the center at a time. One child acts as the post office worker while the other two children act as customers. Using the coins, have each customer buy stamps, envelopes, and valentines (or buy paper to make his own valentine). The post office worker takes the money and gives change to the customer. The customer uses the items to make a valentine for someone in the class and then places his valentine in the cardboard mailbox. On or before Valentine's Day, have youngsters assist you in delivering the mail!

Kaye Sowell—Gr. K
Pelahatchie Elementary School
Pelahatchie, MS

A Country Store

A shopping spree at this store is rich in learning experiences. To make the store, spray paint the inside and outside of an old trunk. (White works best for the inside color.) When the paint is dry, use wood glue to mount strips of wood to serve as shelf rests. Cover shelves with adhesive covering; then place them inside the trunk. Attach a price sticker (appropriately priced for your youngsters' level) to each item in a supply of empty commercial food containers. Then stock the shelves with the priced merchandise and a cash register with real or play money. Post an Open/Closed sign and the name of the store on the trunk. During centers time, open the trunk and put the cash register on a small table or countertop. To use this center, encourage youngsters to engage in creative dramatic play including buying the merchandise and exchanging money. At closing time, everything fits neatly inside the closed trunk.

Kathleen Miller—Gr. K
Our Lady Of Mt. Carmel School
Tenafly, NJ

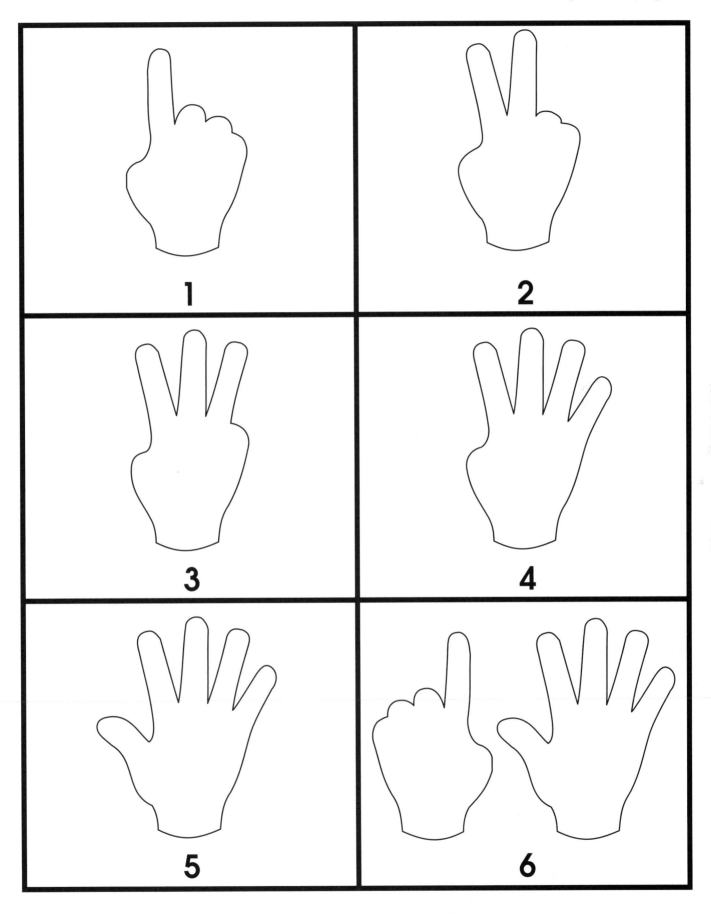

1

2

3

4

5

6

Turtle Patterns
Use with "Get Your
Turtles In A Row"
on page 97.

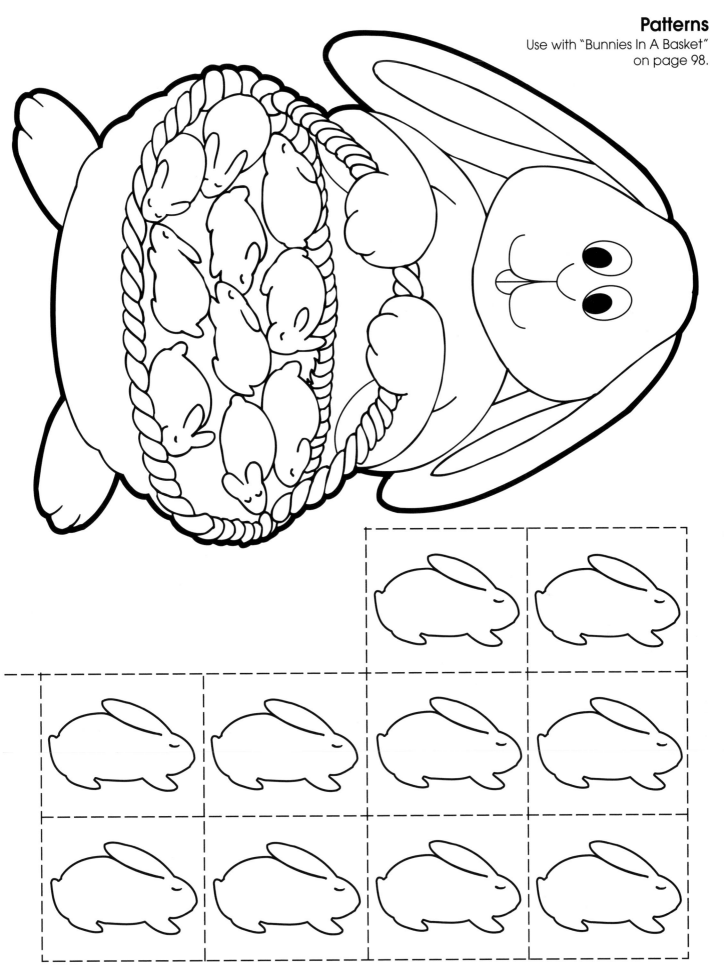

Name _____

Graph the Easter eggs by color.

Math Tips

Graph Paper Shapes

Your students' knowledge of squares will shape up quickly when you use graph paper. Using a piece of graph paper with black lines, draw several different-sized squares. Duplicate a copy for each child and have him count and label the number of spaces on the sides of each square. When he realizes the number of spaces on all four sides is the same, the concept of a square will really take shape for him.

Audrey Teller
Sterling Elementary School
Sterling Heights, MI

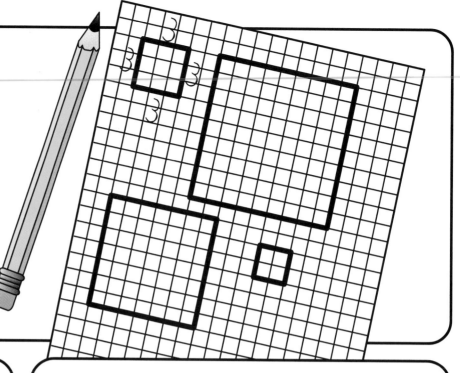

Shape Reinforcement

Reinforce shapes with this large-group activity. When you call youngsters together for group time, ask them to sit in a square, triangle, rectangle, or circle. You'll see shape recognition take shape fast!

Connie Allen—Gr. K
Immanuel Lutheran School
Manitowoc, WI

Place "Mat-nipulatives"

Create an assortment of colorful, durable "mat-nipulatives" from vinyl place mats. Cut old vinyl place mats into different shapes of varying sizes. Place the shapes in a decorated container at a center. Youngsters can classify the shapes by color, size, or shape or can use them as counters. For added fun, attach a strip of magnetic tape to the back of each shape and allow youngsters to manipulate the shapes on the chalkboard or other magnetic surface.

Pat Bollinger—Gr. K
Leopold R-3
Leopold, MO

Tiling Tactics

Team up with ceramic tiles to create a variety of center activities. Cut apart the tiles from sheets of one-inch floor tiling. Place the tiles in a box at a center and have youngsters use them for counting, sorting, and tracing activities. For a patterning activity, glue tiles to poster-board cards and have youngsters reproduce the patterns using additional tiles. For a more challenging activity, a youngster creates a design and then reproduces it by gluing matching one-inch construction-paper squares to a sheet of paper. Whichever tactic you choose, you're sure to agree that these durable manipulatives are terrific!

Robin Gorman—Gr. K
Potterville Elementary
Potterville, MI

Reusable Graph

Convert an old chalkboard or sheet of plywood into a reusable graph. Cover the chalkboard or plywood with Con-Tact® paper if desired; then attach several horizontal rows of magnetic tape squares. Laminate several poster-board strips and attach a strip of magnetic tape to the back of each one. Glue a happy face cutout inside a juice can lid for each youngster. Near the graph, place a bucket containing the strips, lids, and a wipe-off pen. When it's time to graph, program the needed strips and attach them to the graph. Then ask each youngster to place a lid on the graph to indicate his preference. When the graph is complete, have youngsters interpret the information; then wipe off the strips and replace the strips and lids in the bucket. Graphing has never been easier!

Betty L. Gomillion
South Leake Elementary
Walnut Grove, MS

Our Favorite Ice Cream

| chocolate | | | | |
| vanilla | | | | |

Instant Graphing

A little advance preparation makes graphing activities a snap. Program sheets of poster board with vertical and horizontal bargraph grids. Then program a two-inch poster board square for each child with his name and a photocopy of his school picture. Laminate the grids and squares for durability. When it's time to graph, use a wipe-off marker to program a grid. Then have each child tape his square to the appropriate section of the grid to create a bar graph. When the information is no longer needed, simply remove the squares and wipe off the programming. In a snap, your graph is clean and ready to use again.

Lisa Heintz—Gr. K
St. Mary School
Cincinnati, OH

Josh

Favorite Colors

red				
yellow				
blue				
green				
orange				
purple				

Favorite Pets

dog | cat | fish | horse | hamster | bird | gerbil

Graphing Board

Transform a science display board (or any large freestanding piece of cardboard) into a versatile graphing board. Cover the board with a solid color of adhesive covering. Use colored tape to make the grid. Label the rows and/or columns using a permanent marker. To graph results, have each youngster tape a personalized cutout in the appropriate place. To change the labels, wipe the original labels off with a spritz of hairspray.

Phyllis Monroe—Gr. K
Vandalia Elementary School
Greensboro, NC

Do you like pumpkin pie?

Sara	
Lea	
Janie	Katlin
Paul	A. J.
Sonny	Zack
Yes	No

David
Joe
Julie
Amy
Val

Eva
Jack

Collections To Sort

Need a collection of manipulatives for sorting, counting, and patterning? If so, here's a foolproof way to keep your classroom well stocked. Several days prior to Open House, send home a letter asking students to bring collections of small objects such as buttons, keys, hair barrettes, or shells. Have youngsters bring the items on the night of Open House. Place several empty baskets on a designated table for each child to sort his items into.

Robin Gorman—Gr. K
Potterville Elementary
Potterville, MI

Seasonal Borders

Involve students in bulletin-board construction by providing them with a roll of blank adding-machine tape, seasonal sponges, and paint. Announce the theme of the bulletin board and have your students decorate the paper strips appropriately using sponges and paint. If desired, have students decide on a pattern to be repeated on the strips. Use the completed strip as an eye-catching border.

Kathleen McCarthy—Gr. K
Frankfurt American Elementary School
Frankfurt, Germany

Detergent Scoops

You know those measuring scoops that come in powdered detergent boxes—well, use 'em at home; then bring 'em to school! They make great containers when children need an individual glue supply or other art supplies. They also can be used for sorting or counting activities. Label each cup with a numeral or picture; then have children place the appropriate items or counters in the cups.

Debra S. Bott—Gr. K
Duson Elementary
Scott, LA

Bingo Sponge-Markers

Colorful bingo sponge-markers (available at discount stores) lend themselves to a variety of learning activities. Have youngsters use the markers to make sets and patterns, create art pictures, and explore color combinations. The possibilities go on and on!

Cheryl Lynn Trost—Gr. K
Wolfridge Elementary
Bunker Hill, IL

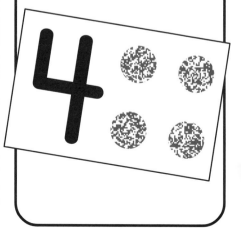

New Twist On 100 Days

Keep count of the first 100 days of school and practice patterning skills at the same time. Each day as you start your daily routine, glue a symbol (such as a letter, numeral, shape, or picture) on a sentence strip. As school days go by, add symbols to the strip to create a pattern. When the first strip has ten symbols, start another strip with a different pattern. Continue in this manner until the 100th day of school. This is a great way to reinforce counting and patterning skills.

Cynthia Goodrich
Forestbrook Elementary
Myrtle Beach, SC

Hundred Hats

Dress up your 100th-day festivities with Hundred Hats. For each hat you will need large numeral cutouts to make "100" and a construction-paper strip the correct length for a headband. Have a child write the numeral 100 several times on the headband, then staple it. Attach the numeral cutouts to the front of the headband.

Barbara Pasley—Grs. K–1 Special Ed.
Energy Elementary
Energy, IL

Noteworthy Numbers

Here's a number recognition activity youngsters will be sure to take note of. Each time you introduce a new number, have each youngster glue an identical number of construction paper shapes atop a corresponding 12-inch, construction-paper cutout. For extra number-recognition practice, have each youngster take his cutout home and display it on his refrigerator. Youngsters identify the numbers each time they open their refrigerators, counting the shapes for self-checking.

Ellyn Soypher—Preschool
Chizuk Amuno Nursery School
Baltimore, MD

Miniblind Bonanza

Create durable learning activities using extra slats from vinyl miniblinds. Cut the slats into various lengths and program them with a permanent marker to create:

- number and set matching pairs
- desktags
- alphabet-sequencing activities
- number-sequencing activities
- size-seriation manipulatives.

Valerie Bishel
Rustburg, VA

Table Time

Make the most of the round tables in your classroom with this timely idea. Cut the numerals 1 through 12 out of colorful Con-Tact® paper. Attach them to a tabletop to create a clock face. To make the hands, cut two circles, an hour hand, and a minute hand out of poster board. Place the ends of the two hands between the circles and connect all four layers with a paper fastener. Tape only the bottom circle to the center of the table so that the hands of the clock can be moved. Direct each tableful of children to work cooperatively to "set" their clocks during various times of the day. For a quick game, direct one child at each table to position the hands while his tablemates watch and tell the time.

Cynthia Donnelly, Kensington Avenue School, Springfield, MA

Coin Counting

You can bank on money skills improving with this coin-counting activity. Keep a supply of overhead coins or large bulletin-board coins handy. Whenever you need a quick time-filler, show youngsters a combination of coins and have them count the coins to determine the total. If they are able, have youngsters take turns displaying the sets of coins as their classmates count the totals.

Peggy Taylor—Gr. K
South Central Elementary
Union Mills, IN

Clock Pillow

Combine fine-motor skills and telling time for hours of hands-on fun. Sew twelve shank-style buttons onto a round pillow to resemble a clock face. Program each button with the appropriate number. Sew another button to the center of the pillow; then button on two felt clock hands that have buttonholes near both ends. Youngsters manipulate the clock hands and button them in place. It's six o'clock on the button!

Debi Hussell
Central Elementary
Point Pleasant, NV

Telling Time

Do your students get confused with minute and hour hands when learning to tell time? Children can easily discriminate between the two hands if you provide them with a simple clock reminder. To make each child his own clock, number a paper plate to resemble a clock face. Cut two arrow cutouts from tagboard, making one longer than the other. Label the hour hand with the child's first name and the minute hand with the child's last name. Fasten the two arrow cutouts to the paper plate with a brad. Provide each student with his own clock and explain that the number you say first when telling time is the number your first name is pointing to (hour hand). The number you say last is the number your last name is pointing to (minute hand). This is sure to take the guesswork out of doing clock work.

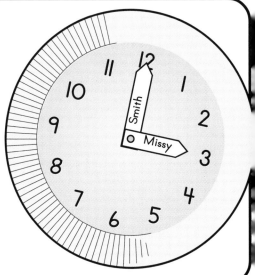

Melissa Smith—Gr. K
Collegiate School
Passaic, NJ

Index Of Ideas